Imágenes

Student Activities Manual

Student Activities Manual
Workbook / Lab Manual
Second Edition

Imágenes

An Introduction to Spanish Language and Cultures

Debbie Rusch
Boston College

Marcela Domínguez
University of Southern California

Lucía Caycedo Garner
University of Wisconsin–Madison, Emerita

Australia • Brazil • Japan • Korea • Mexico • Singapore • Spain • United Kingdom • United States

Imágenes: An Introduction to Spanish Language and Cultures, Student Activities Manual, Second Edition
Debbie Rusch, Marcela Domínguez, and Lucía Caycedo Garner

Publisher: Rolando Hernández

Development Editor: Sandra Guadano

Project Editor: Harriet C. Dishman / Michael E. Packard

Director of Manufacturing: Priscilla Manchester

Executive Marketing Director: Eileen Bernadette Moran

Associate Marketing Manager: Claudia Martínez

Credits

Page 19, © *Vanidades Continental*; page 19, courtesy of Humberto Hincapié Villegas; page 37, http://www.plus.es/codigo/television/television.asp; page 69, Excerpt on "Machu Picchu" from http://traficoperu.com/machupicchu.htm; page 69, Excerpt on "Hiram Bingham" from http://www.infoweb.com.pe/villarreal/fdcp0f.htm; page 85 (top), © Nevada Wier/CORBIS; page 85 (bottom), © Tony Arruza/CORBIS; page 101 (top and bottom) courtesy of author; page 116, © Robert Fried; page 122, courtesy of Mi Buenos Aires Querido; page 167, Copyright © 1986 by Houghton Mifflin Company. Adapted and reproduced by permission from *The American Heritage Spanish Dictionary*; page 179, © Mary Altier; page 190, from "El Mundo a Su Alcance con Hertz," reprinted by permission of the Hertz Corporation.

Illustrations

Andrés Fernandez Cordón: pages 12, 14, 210, 222 (top)

Mark Heng: pages 57, 131, 187, 191, 217

Tim Jones: pages 90, 241

Len Shalansky: pages 6, 121, 183(a), 204, 229, 239

Doug Wilcox: pages 222 (bottom), 248

Will Winslow: pages 4, 5, 29, 46, 49, 50, 68, 76, 78, 79, 111, 130, 139, 186, 202, 203, 207, 211, 212, 214, 216, 225, 240, 245, 258

Joyce A. Zarins: pages 44, 62, 64, 67, 140, 143, 160, 183(b&c), 213, 219, 220, 228, 230, 231, 252, 256

For product information and technology assistance, contact us at
Cengage Learning Customer & Sales Support, 1-800-354-9706

For permission to use material from this text or product,
submit all requests online at **www.cengage.com/permissions**
Further permissions questions can be emailed to
permissionrequest@cengage.com

ISBN-13: 978-0-618-66042-1

ISBN-10: 0-618-66042-9

Heinle
20 Channel Center Street
Boston, MA 02210
USA

Cengage Learning is a leading provider of customized learning solutions with office locations around the globe, including Singapore, the United Kingdom, Australia, Mexico, Brazil, and Japan. Locate your local office at **www.cengage.com/global**

Cengage Learning products are represented in Canada by Nelson Education, Ltd.

To learn more about Heinle, visit **www.cengage.com/heinle**

Purchase any of our products at your local college store or at our preferred online store **www.ichapters.com**

Printed in the United States of America
9 10 11 12 13 13 12 11 10

Contents

To the Student

The Student Activities Manual to accompany ***Imágenes,*** *Second Edition* is divided in two parts: Workbook Activities and Lab Manual Activities.

Workbook

The Workbook activities are designed to reinforce the chapter material and to help develop your writing skills. Each chapter in the Workbook parallels the organization of your textbook so that you can begin doing the activities after studying each **Vocabulario esencial** and **Gramática para la comunicación** section in the text.

Un poco de todo sections in the middle and at the end of each chapter include activities that focus on more than one concept. This helps you apply your learning to more real-life like situations in which multiple topics come into play at once. At the end of the chapter, reading activities reinforce the strategies introduced in the textbook as you read about the Hispanic world. Becoming a better reader can also help you in other aspects of the language, such as increasing your vocabulary.

The **Repaso** sections after odd-numbered chapters will help you review some key concepts and are especially useful for review prior to midterm or final exams.

Answers to the Workbook activities may be made available to you by your instructor.

Here are some tips to follow when using the Workbook:

- Before doing the exercises, study the corresponding vocabulary and grammar sections in the textbook.
- Do the exercises with the textbook closed and without looking at the answer key.
- Write what you have learned. Be creative, but not overly so. Try not to overstep your linguistic boundaries.
- Try to use dictionaries sparingly.
- Check your answers against the answer key, if provided by your instructor, marking all incorrect answers in a different color ink.
- Check any wrong answers against the grammar explanations and vocabulary lists in the textbook. Make notes to yourself in the margins to use as study aids.
- Use your notes to help prepare for exams and quizzes.
- If you feel you need additional work with particular portions of the chapter, do the corresponding exercises in the CD-ROM or on the ***Imágenes*** Website.

Lab Manual

The activities in the Lab Manual are designed to help improve your pronunciation and listening skills. Each chapter contains two main parts:

- **Mejora tu pronunciación:** Contains an explanation of the sounds and rhythm of Spanish, followed by pronunciation exercises. This section can be done at the beginning of a chapter.
- **Mejora tu comprensión:** Contains numerous listening comprehension activities. As you listen to these recordings, you will be given a task to perform (for example, completing a telephone message as you hear the conversation). This section should be done after studying the last grammar explanation. It will help prepare you for the listening comprehension sections of the exams and quizzes.

The audio program for each chapter ends with the corresponding conversations from the text, which you may also listen to on the audio CD packaged with the textbook or on the ***Imágenes*** Website.

Tips for improving pronunciation and listening skills:

- While doing the pronunciation exercises, listen carefully, repeat accurately, and speak up.
- Read all directions and items before doing the listening comprehension activities.
- Pay specific attention to the setting and type of spoken language (for example, an announcement in a store, a radio newscast, a conversation between two students about exams, and so forth).
- Do not be concerned with understanding every word; your goal should be to do the task that is asked of you in the activity.
- Replay the activities as many times as needed.
- Listen to the recordings again after correction to hear what you missed.

Conscientious use of the Workbook and Lab Manual will help you make good progress in your study of the Spanish language. Should you need or want additional practice, the CD-ROM and Website exercises are excellent review tools for quizzes and exams.

Workbook

Nombre ______________________ Sección ______________ Fecha ____________

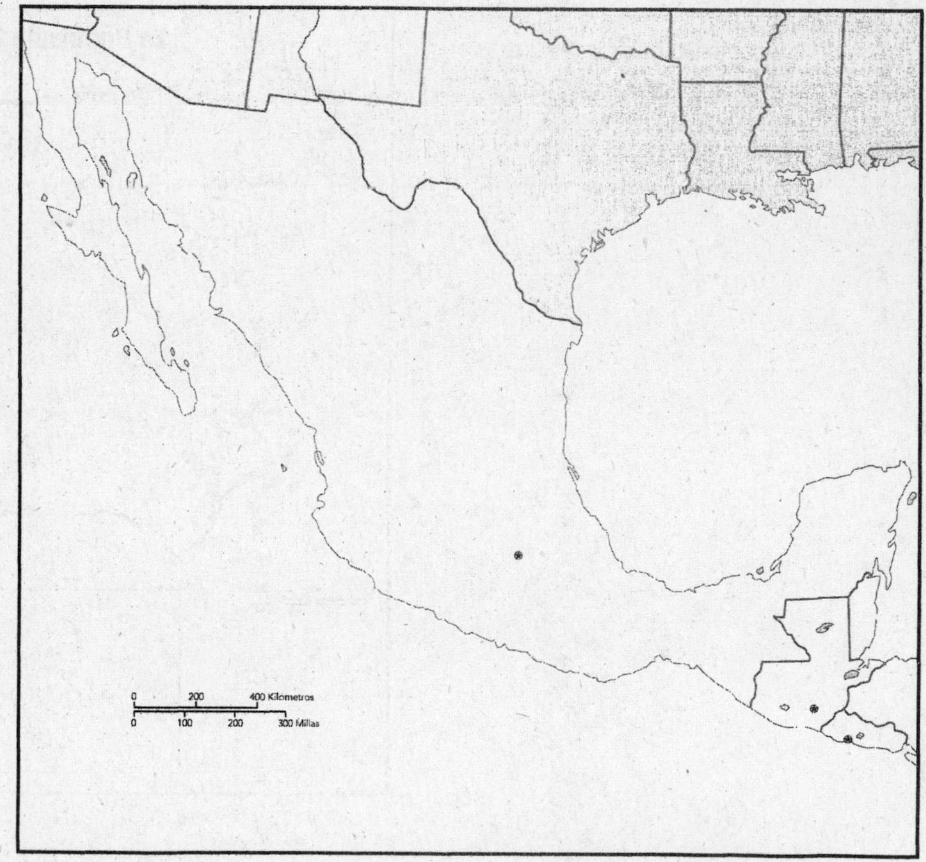

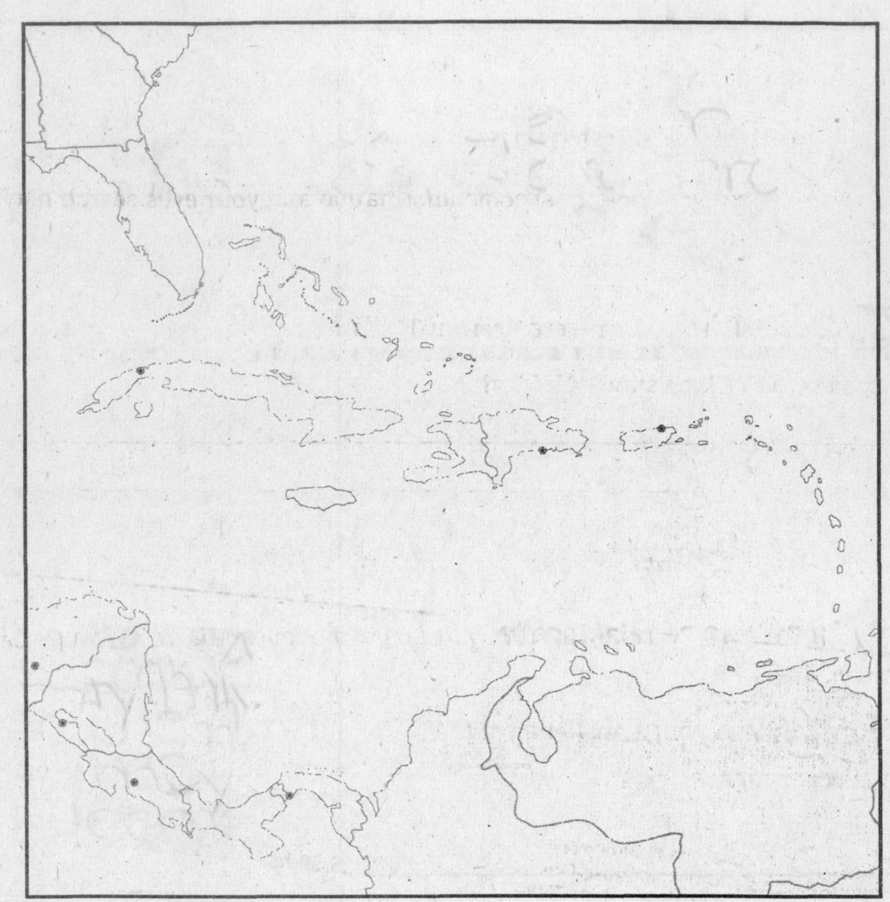

Nombre ______________________ Sección ______________ Fecha ____________

Lectura

Estrategia de lectura: Scanning

When scanning a written text, you look for specific information and your eyes search like radar beams for their target.

Actividad 27 **La televisión.** Scan these Spanish TV listings to answer the following question:

¿Cuáles son los programas de los Estados Unidos?

____

____

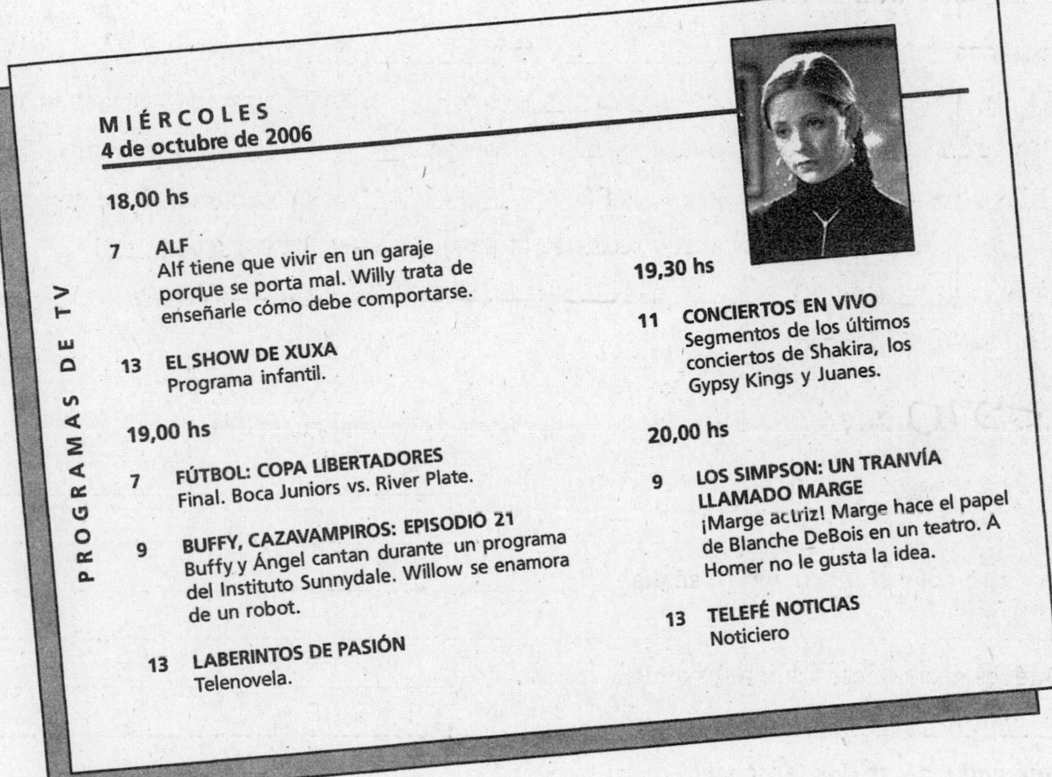

PROGRAMAS DE TV

MIÉRCOLES
4 de octubre de 2006

18,00 hs

7 **ALF**
Alf tiene que vivir en un garaje porque se porta mal. Willy trata de enseñarle cómo debe comportarse.

13 **EL SHOW DE XUXA**
Programa infantil.

19,00 hs

7 **FÚTBOL: COPA LIBERTADORES**
Final. Boca Juniors vs. River Plate.

9 **BUFFY, CAZAVAMPIROS: EPISODIO 21**
Buffy y Ángel cantan durante un programa del Instituto Sunnydale. Willow se enamora de un robot.

13 **LABERINTOS DE PASIÓN**
Telenovela.

19,30 hs

11 **CONCIERTOS EN VIVO**
Segmentos de los últimos conciertos de Shakira, los Gypsy Kings y Juanes.

20,00 hs

9 **LOS SIMPSON: UN TRANVÍA LLAMADO MARGE**
¡Marge actriz! Marge hace el papel de Blanche DeBois en un teatro. A Homer no le gusta la idea.

13 **TELEFÉ NOTICIAS**
Noticiero

Nombre Andrea Busalacchi Sección 103 Fecha ____________

Capítulo

4 ¿Tarde o temprano?

100

Vocabulario esencial I

Las partes del cuerpo

Actividad 1 **¿Qué parte es?** Look at the following drawing and label the parts of the body. Be sure to include the definite article.

1. la cabeza
2. el ojo
3. la nariz
4. ____________
5. la boca
6. la boca
7. el dedo
8. la mano
9. el brazo
10. el codo
11. el estomago
12. la rodilla
13. la pierna
14. el pie
15. las nalgas
16. la espalda
17. el hombre
18. el cuello
19. la oreja
20. ____________

Actividad 2 **La parte más interesante.** Stars are constantly scrutinized for their appearance, either in a positive or a negative manner. Associate these people with their most distinctive body part; then write if you like it or not. If you don't, indicate what that person should do to improve. Here are a few suggestions for what they should do: **consultar con un cirujano plástico, ir al dentista, hacer ejercicio, ir a un peluquero** (*hair stylist / barber*) **bueno, comprar una peluca** (*wig*).

➤ nariz / Matt Damon ***Me gusta la nariz de Matt Damon. ¡Qué sexy/bonita/atractiva!***
No me gusta la nariz de Matt Damon. ¡Qué fea/horrible/gorda!
Debe consultar con un cirujano plástico.

1. pelo / Donald Trump
2. dientes / Madonna
3. piernas / Anna Kournikova
4. estómago / Kirsty Ally
5. labios / Mick Jagger
6. barba / Billy Gibbons de ZZ Top
7. boca / Julia Roberts
8. orejas / el príncipe Carlos de Inglaterra
9. ojos / Renée Zellweger

Acciones reflexivas

Actividad 3 **Los verbos reflexivos.** Select the word that does not belong in each of the following groups.

1. bañarse, lavarse, levantarse, ducharse
2. la barba, el bigote, afeitarse, quitarse la ropa
3. cepillarse, maquillarse, pelo, peinarse
4. el jabón, lavarse la cara, afeitarse, ducharse
5. ducharse, el pelo, cepillarse, los dientes
6. quitarse, ponerse, la ropa, lavarse

Nombre ______________________ Sección ______________ Fecha ____________

Actividad 4 **Asociaciones.** Write all the reflexive actions that you associate with each of the following items.

➤ los dientes *cepillarse*

1. la cara ______________________
2. la barba ______________________
3. la ropa ______________________
4. las manos ______________________
5. el cuerpo ______________________
6. los ojos ______________________
7. las piernas ______________________

Gramática para la comunicación I

Describing Daily Routines: Reflexive Verbs

Actividad 5 **Las rutinas.** Complete the following sentences with the appropriate form of the indicated reflexive verbs.

1. Los domingos yo ________ ________ tarde. (levantarse)
2. Mi novio no ________ ________ porque a mí me gusta la barba. (afeitarse)
3. Todos los niños ________ ________ el pelo con champú Johnson para no llorar. (lavarse)
4. Nosotros siempre ________ ________ tarde. (levantarse)
5. ¿________ ________ o ________ ________ tú por la mañana? (ducharse, bañarse)
6. Yo ________ ________ los dientes después de comer. (cepillarse)
7. El niño tiene cuatro años, pero ________ ________ la ropa solo. (ponerse)
8. Las actrices de Hollywood ________ ________ mucho. (maquillarse)

Actividad 6 **Posición de los reflexivos.** Write the following sentences a different way by changing the position of the reflexive pronoun, but without changing their meaning. Remember to use accents if needed.

1. Voy a lavarme el pelo. ______________________
2. Ella tiene que maquillarse. ______________________
3. Juan se va a afeitar. ______________________
4. Tenemos que levantarnos temprano. ______________________
5. Me estoy poniendo la ropa. ______________________

Actividad 7 **¡Qué tonto!** Rewrite the following nonsense sentences in a logical manner, changing whatever elements are necessary.

1. El señor se afeita los brazos.
____
2. La señora se maquilla el pelo.
____
3. Me levanto, me pongo la ropa y me ducho.
____
4. Antes de comer, los chicos se quitan las manos.
____
5. Antes de salir de la casa, me cepillo la nariz y me maquillo las orejas.
____

Actividad 8 **Una familia extraña.** Pedro's family seems to be caught in a routine. First read the entire paragraph, then go back and fill in the missing words with the appropriate forms of the verbs in the list. You can use verbs more than once. When finished, reread the paragraph and check to see that each verb agrees with its subject. Note: Some verbs are reflexives and some aren't.

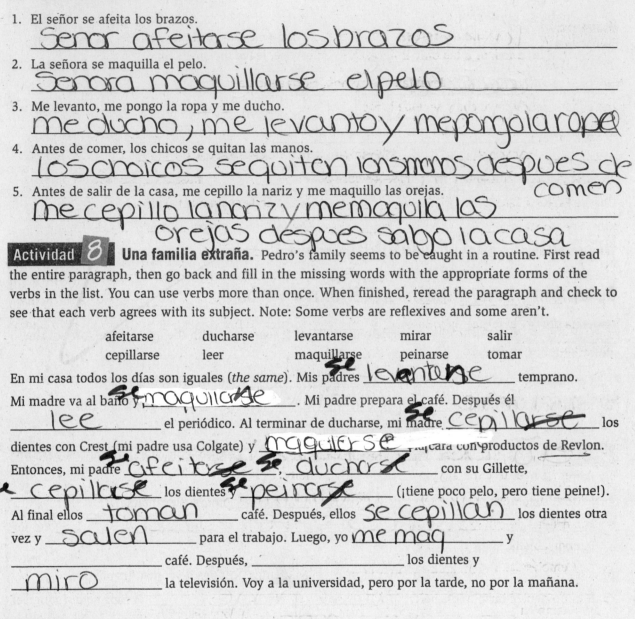

afeitarse	ducharse	levantarse	mirar	salir
cepillarse	leer	maquillarse	peinarse	tomar

En mi casa todos los días son iguales (*the same*). Mis padres ______________ temprano. Mi madre va al baño y ______________. Mi padre prepara el café. Después él ______________ el periódico. Al terminar de ducharse, mi madre ______________ los dientes con Crest (mi padre usa Colgate) y ______________ la cara con productos de Revlon. Entonces, mi padre ______________, ______________ con su Gillette, ______________ los dientes y ______________ (¡tiene poco pelo, pero tiene peine!). Al final ellos ______________ café. Después, ellos ______________ los dientes otra vez y ______________ para el trabajo. Luego, yo ______________ y ______________ café. Después, ______________ los dientes y ______________ la televisión. Voy a la universidad, pero por la tarde, no por la mañana.

The Personal *a*

Actividad 9 ***A, al, a la, a los, a las.*** Complete the following sentences with **a, al, a la, a los,** or **a las** only if necessary; otherwise, leave the space blank.

1. Voy a ir ______________ ciudad.
2. No veo bien ______________ actor.
3. ¿______________ ti te gusta esquiar?
4. Escucho ______________ discos compactos muy interesantes.
5. Tengo ______________ un profesor muy interesante.
6. Siempre visitamos ______________ padres de mi novio.

Continued on next page →

Nombre ______________________ Sección ______________ Fecha ______________

7. Vamos a ver a la película mañana.
8. Me gustar caminar al parque.

Actividad 10 **El día de Teresa.** Finish the following paragraph about what Teresa is doing today. Use **a, al, a la, a los,** or **a las** only if necessary; otherwise, leave the space blank.

Hoy Teresa va a levantarse temprano. Normalmente escucha — CDs de salsa y merengue cuando se ducha y se pone la ropa. Después va a la universidad. Hoy tiene que ver al profesor Aguirre para hablar sobre un examen. Por la tarde va a llamar a Álvaro y a Diana para tomar un café con ellos. A Álvaro le gusta la cafetería Nueva Orleans porque siempre ponen la música vieja de John Coltrane, Charlie Parker y Ella Fitzgerald. Pero a Teresa no le gusta mucho escuchar al jazz. Por eso van a ir la cafetería Teatriz porque es más tranquila. Después Teresa tiene que ir ______ Biblioteca Nacional para hacer ______ investigación para una clase. Más tarde tiene que ir a la oficina de su tío Alejandro para hablar un poco del trabajo. Por la noche, a Teresa le gustaría ir ______ bailar. ______ amigos de Teresa les gusta mucho el reggaetón y tienen ______ música de Don Omar y Tego Calderón, pero Daddy Yankee es su favorito.

Un poco de todo

Actividad 11 **Una carta.** Finish the following letter to your Spanish-speaking grandmother, who has asked you to describe a typical day at the university.

Universidad de Alverno, 12 de septiembre de 20 11

Querida abuela:

¿Cómo estás? Yo estoy. Me gusta mucho la clase de espanol. Estudio mucho pero también correr. Tengo muchos amigos que son guapa y alta. A ellos les gusta mirar las peliculas.

Todos los días son iguales; normalmente me levanto y me cepillo losdientes y me maquillo. Después de clase, llamo por teléfono a mi novio. Y por la noche como en la cafeteria.

Un abrazo (*hug*),

Andrea

(tu nombre)

Vocabulario esencial II

Los meses, las estaciones, el tiempo y las fechas

Actividad 12 **Las fechas y las estaciones.** Write out the following dates and state what season it is in the Northern and Southern Hemispheres. Remember that the day is written first in Spanish. The first one has been done for you.

	Fecha	Hemisferio norte	Hemisferio sur
a. 15/2	el quince de febrero	invierno	verano
b. 3/4	el trec de marzo	otono	primavera
c. 15/12	el quince d deciembre	verano	invierno
d. 30/8	la treinta de agosto	inverno	verano
e. 25/10	viente y cinco de octubre	primavera	otono
f. 1/2	uno de febrero	verano	invierno

Actividad 13 **El tiempo.** Look at the accompanying drawings. Using complete sentences, state what the weather is like in each case. The first one has been done for you.

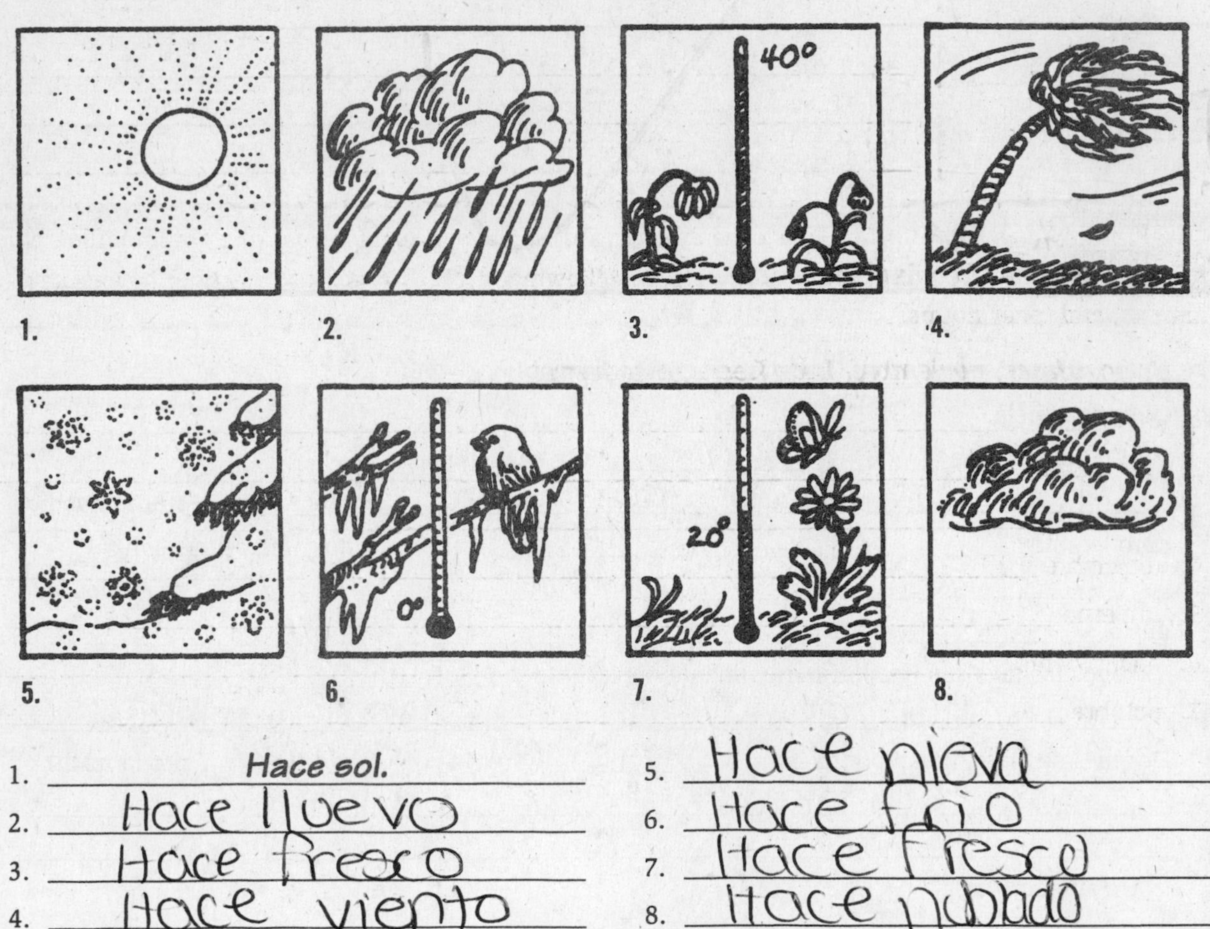

1. *Hace sol.*
2. Hace lluevo
3. Hace fresco
4. Hace viento
5. Hace nieva
6. Hace frio
7. Hace fresco
8. Hace nublado

Nombre ______________________ Sección ______________ Fecha ______________

Actividad 14 **Fechas importantes.** Complete the following lists with names, events, and dates (e.g., **el doce de marzo**) that are important to you.

		Fecha
Cumpleaños:	madre	es el seis de marzo
	padre	es el siete de julio
	Me	es el dos de enero
	Hijo	es el cuatro de mayo
	Novio	es el trientaiuno de agusto
Aniversario:	padres	es el veinticinco de abril
Último (*Last*) día de clases:	SC119	es el circuenta de mayo
Exámenes finales:	español	es ed doce de mayo
	cm112	es el dies de mayo
	Algebra	es el dies de mayo
	Sc119	es el circuenta de mayo
	PN120	es el circuenta de mayo

Actividad 15 **Asociaciones.** Associate the following words with actions, weather expressions, months, and other nouns.

➤ otoño ***clases, noviembre, hace fresco, estudiamos***

1. julio hace sol, hace calor,
2. primavera hace fresco, hace viento, abril
3. Acapulco hace sol, hace buen tiempo
4. diciembre hace mal tiempo, hace nieva
5. invierno enero, hace frio, es mi cumpleanos
6. hacer viento el inviemo, hace fresco
7. octubre hace fio, el ontono

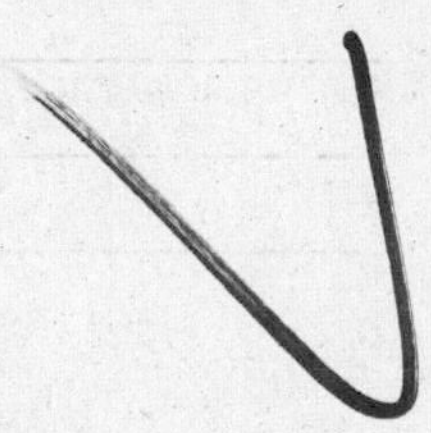

Actividad 16 **¿Qué tiempo hace?** You are on vacation in the Dominican Republic, and you call a friend in Cleveland. As always, you begin your conversation by talking about the weather. Complete the following conversation based on the accompanying drawings.

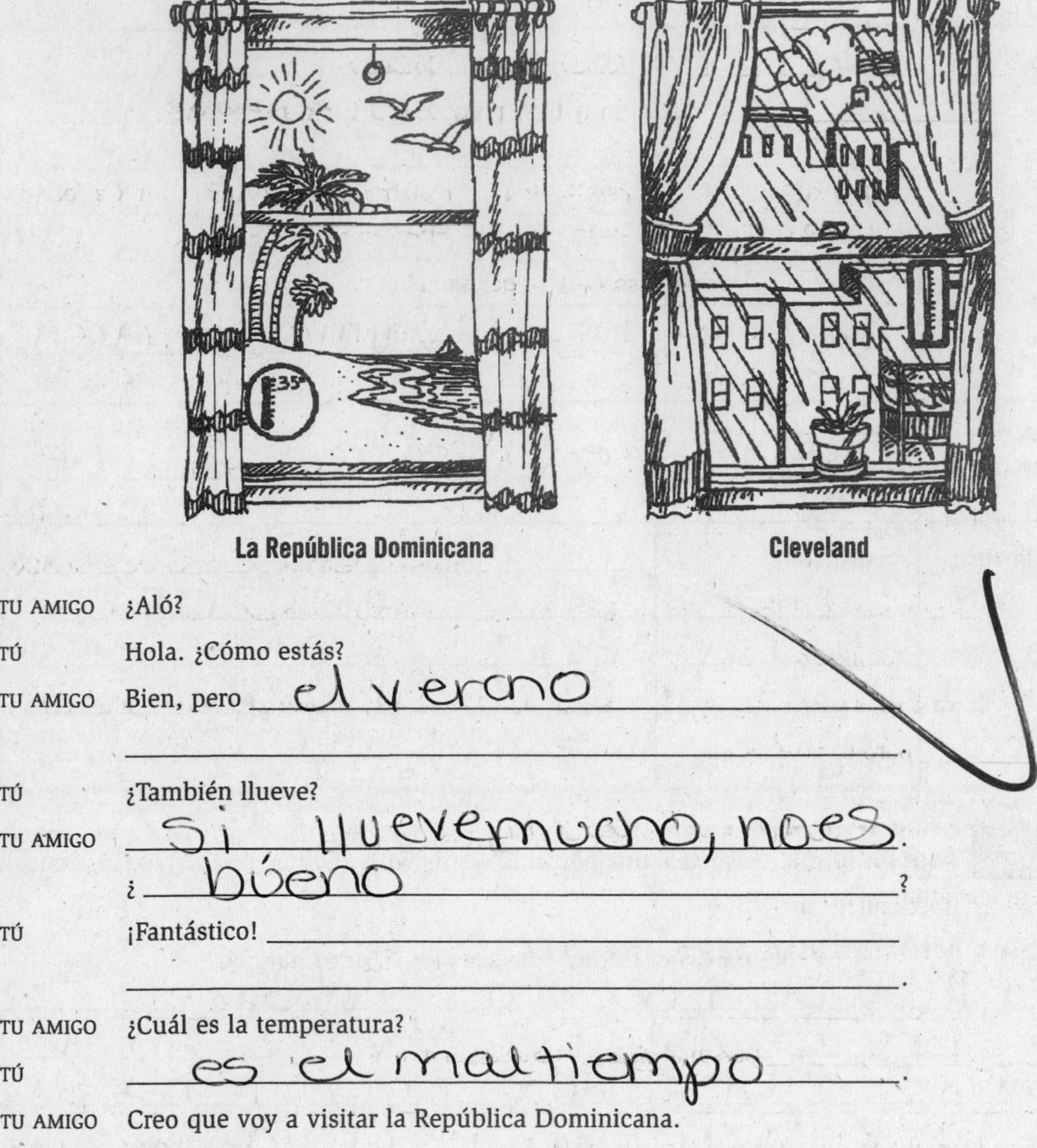

La República Dominicana **Cleveland**

TU AMIGO ¿Aló?

TÚ Hola. ¿Cómo estás?

TU AMIGO Bien, pero el verano ______________________________.

TÚ ¿También llueve?

TU AMIGO Si lluevemucho, noes ¿búeno?

TÚ ¡Fantástico! ______________________________.

TU AMIGO ¿Cuál es la temperatura?

TÚ es el maltiempo.

TU AMIGO Creo que voy a visitar la República Dominicana.

Gramática para la comunicación II

Talking about Who and What You Know: *Saber* and *conocer*

Actividad 17 ***¿Saber* o *conocer?*** Complete the following sentences with the appropriate form of the verbs **saber** or **conocer**.

1. ¿ conoces tú a mi padre?
2. Yo no Se tu número de teléfono.

Continued on next page →

Nombre ______________________________ Sección ______________ Fecha ____________

3. ¿______________________ Uds. dónde está la casa de Fernanda?
4. Ellos ______________________ Caracas muy bien porque trabajan allí.
5. ¿______________________ nadar Teresa?
6. ¿______________________ Uds. cómo se llama el profesor nuevo?
7. Yo no ______________________ la película nueva de Almodóvar.
8. Jorge ______________________ bailar muy bien porque es bailarín profesional.

Actividad 18 **Claudia y sus amigos.** Finish the following story about Claudia, Juan Carlos, Vicente, and Teresa. Fill in the blanks with the correct form of **saber** or **conocer.**

Claudia desea ______________ más de Juan Carlos; por eso llama a Teresa porque ella ______________ a Juan Carlos. Teresa ______________ que Juan Carlos va a llamar a Claudia para salir con ella. Teresa también ______________ que a Juan Carlos le gusta ir a discotecas y que ______________ bailar salsa muy bien. Él ______________ una discoteca que se llama *Son Latino*, pero Teresa no ______________ exactamente dónde está.

Vicente también ______________ a Juan Carlos. Claudia ______________ que a Teresa le gusta mucho Vicente. Teresa no ______________ su número de teléfono, pero ella ve a Vicente todos los días en la cafetería. Entonces, mañana Teresa va a hablar con Vicente para ir al cine con Claudia y Juan Carlos el domingo.

Así que Teresa va a salir con Vicente y Claudia con Juan Carlos. ¿Va a pasar algo interesante? Quién ______________ pero es posible...

Actividad 19 **Muchas preguntas pero poco dinero.** You work for a low-budget advertising agency that makes ads for TV and radio. Complete your boss's questions, using **saber** or **conocer,** and then answer them in complete sentences.

1. ¿______________ el número de teléfono de la compañía de champú?
____
2. ¿Tú ______________ personalmente a un actor famoso?
____
3. Necesito un pianista para un anuncio comercial (*ad*). ¿______________ tocar el piano?
____
4. Necesito un fotógrafo. ¿______________ a un fotógrafo bueno?
____
5. ¿______________ tus amigos nuestros productos?
____

Pointing Out: Demonstrative Adjectives and Pronouns

Actividad 20 **¿Cuál es?** Complete these miniconversations by selecting the appropriate demonstrative and writing the correct form.

1. —Me gustan las plantas que están cerca de la puerta.
   —¿ ______________________ plantas que están allí? (este, ese)
2. —¿Te gustan ______________________ discos compactos que tengo en la mano? (este, aquel)
   —Sí, me gustan mucho.
3. —¿Dónde está el restaurante?
   —Tenemos que caminar mucho. Es ______________________ restaurante que está allá. (este, aquel)
4. —¿Vas a comprar una revista?
   —Sí, pero ¿cuál quieres? ¿ ______________________ que tengo aquí o ______________________ que está allí? (este, ese) (este, ese)
   —Me gusta más *People en español.*

Un poco de todo

Actividad 21 **Lógica.** Finish the following series of words in a logical manner.

1. junio, julio, ______________________
2. hacer frío, hacer fresco, ______________________
3. afeitarse, crema de afeitar; lavarse el pelo, champú; cepillarse los dientes, ______________________
4. este libro, ese libro, ______________________
5. verano, ______________________, ______________________, primavera
6. noviembre, ______________________, enero
7. el brazo, el codo, ______________________, los dedos

Actividad 22 **Una conversación.** Luis calls Marcos on his cell phone. Complete the conversation by selecting the correct response.

LUIS ¿Qué estás haciendo?

MARCOS
a. Te estás duchando.
b. Voy a ir a Ávila mañana.
c. Estoy lavando el carro.

LUIS
a. Yo estoy estudiando y tengo una pregunta.
b. No tengo carro.
c. También estoy duchándome.

Continued on next page →

MARCOS a. Ud. es el profesor.
b. Bueno, pero no sé mucho.
c. Eres experto.

LUIS a. ¡Hombre! Por lo menos sabes más que yo.
b. Claro que soy inteligente.
c. Siempre saca buenas notas.

MARCOS a. O.K. ¿Conoces al profesor?
b. ¿Por qué no hablas con el médico? Sabe mucho.
c. O.K., pero estoy lavando el carro. Más tarde, ¿eh?

Actividad 23 **El fin de semana.** Look at the accompanying map and plan your weekend. You can only go to **one** place. Say where you are going to go and why. Use phrases such as **voy a ir a...**, **porque hace...**, and **me gusta....**

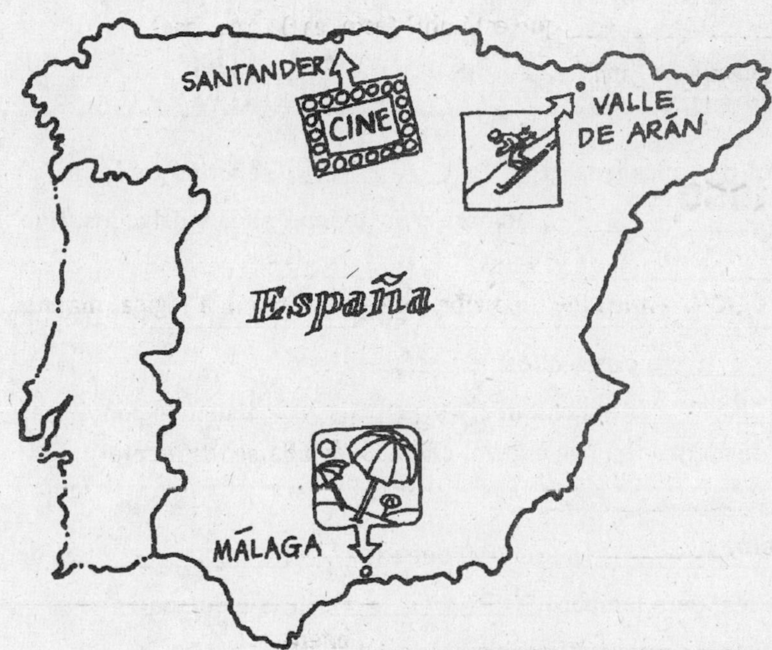

Voy a ir malaga. Porque hace comprar, ir de playa y ir de a la parque.
____
____

Actividad 24 ***La fiesta.*** You and your friend are at a party close to the people on the right and you begin discussing the physical variety that exists among people. Look at the drawing and finish the conversation that follows describing the people you see. Supply the word that is missing for each blank.

TÚ No hay dos personas iguales. ______el______ señor es gordo, bajo y tiene poco pelo. Y ______________ hombres son guapos, altos y delgados. Uno tiene barba y el otro ______________.

TU AMIGA Sí, y ____________________, que ______________ bailando, ______________ muy alto.

TÚ Y ______________ mujer, que ______________ bailando con él, es ______________ también.

TU AMIGA ¿Y aquella señora?

TÚ ¡Huy! ______________ señora, que está ______________, es un poco fea, ¿no?

TU AMIGA No, no es fea, pero tampoco ______________ muy guapa.

TÚ Es verdad, todos somos diferentes.

Lectura

Estrategia de lectura: Using Background Knowledge and Identifying Cognates

The following are excerpts taken from a Peruvian, Spanish-language website about Machu Picchu. By using your general knowledge and your ability to recognize cognates (words in Spanish that are similar to English), you should be able to obtain a great deal of information about this intriguing place.

When doing the following activities, assume that you are a tourist in Peru and do not have a bilingual dictionary. Simply try to get as much information as you can from the readings. A few key words have been glossed to help you.

Nombre ______________________ Sección ______________ Fecha ____________

Actividad 25 **Cognados.** In the excerpts that follow, underline all the cognates (words that are similar in Spanish and English) you can identify and all the words you may have already learned in Spanish. Then read the excerpts to extract as much information as you can.

VISITE MACHU PICCHU

Machu Picchu es, sin duda, el principal atractivo turístico del Perú, y uno de los más renombrados del mundo, atrayendo por este motivo un gran número de turistas anualmente. La UNESCO lo ha declarado Patrimonio Cultural de la Humanidad.

Su arquitectura es el más notable ejemplo inca de integración urbanística con la naturaleza. Esta actitud integral caracterizaba a los incas, y es expresada plenamente en su política estatal, organización social y planificación.

Machu Picchu es un símbolo de peruanidad, que compartimos con toda la humanidad porque presenta los niveles más altos alcanzados por el hombre para vivir integrado armónicamente[1] a su medio ambiente,[2] mediante un avanzado desarrollo tecnológico y estético.

Hiram Bingham

El 14 de julio de 1911, arribó Hiram Bingham con especialistas de la Universidad de Yale en biología, geología, ingeniería y osteología. Ellos fueron conducidos hasta el lugar por Melchor Arteaga, un habitante de la zona quien les dio derroteros[3] de cómo llegar hasta lo que hoy se considera la Octava Maravilla del Mundo.

Posteriormente, en 1914, Bingham volvió a Machu Picchu con apoyo económico y logístico de la propia universidad y la Sociedad Geográfica de los Estados Unidos al frente de un equipo especializado y con una publicación que ya circulaba por el mundo: "La Ciudad Perdida[4] de los Incas".

[1]*in harmony* [2]*environment* [3]*routes* [4]*lost*

Actividad 26 **¿Qué sabes ahora?** Make a list of all the information you have been able to obtain from the above reading. You can make this list in English.

____

____

____

____

____

____

____

____

Nombre ______________________ Sección ______________ Fecha ____________

Capítulo 5 Los planes y las compras

Vocabulario esencial I

La hora, los minutos y los segundos

Actividad 1 **¿Qué hora es?** Write out the following times in complete sentences.

➤ 2:00 ***Son las dos.***

a. 9:15 ______________________

b. 12:05 ______________________

c. 1:25 ______________________

d. 5:40 ______________________

e. 12:45 ______________________

f. 7:30 ______________________

Actividad 2 **La hora.** Answer each of the following questions according to the cue in parentheses. Use complete sentences.

➤ ¿A qué hora vamos a comer? (2:00) ***Vamos a comer a las dos.***

1. ¿A qué hora es la película? (8:30) ______________________
2. ¿Qué hora es? (4:50) ______________________
3. ¿A qué hora es el examen? (10:04) ______________________
4. ¿Cuándo va a llegar el médico? (1:15) ______________________
5. ¿Qué hora es? (12:35) ______________________
6. ¿A qué hora es el programa? (2:45) ______________________

Las sensaciones

Actividad 3 **¿Tiene calor, frío o qué?** Read the following situations and indicate how each person or group of people feels: hot, cold, hungry, etc. Use complete sentences. Remember to use the verb **tener** in your responses.

1. Una persona con una pistola entra en la casa de Esteban. Esteban llama al 911.
   Esteban ______________________________
2. Es el mes de julio y estoy en los Andes chilenos.
   ____
3. Son las tres y media de la mañana y estamos estudiando en la biblioteca.
   ____
4. Estoy en clase y veo mis medias (*socks*). ¡Por Dios! Las dos son de colores diferentes.
   ____
5. Después de jugar al fútbol, Sebastián compra una Coca-Cola.
   Sebastián ______________________________
6. Volvemos de estudiar, vemos una pizzería, entramos y compramos una pizza grande con todo.
   ____
7. Mis amigos están en San Juan, Puerto Rico, en el invierno porque no les gusta el frío de Minnesota.
   Mis amigos ______________________________

Gramática para la comunicación I

Expressing Habitual and Future Actions and Actions in Progress: Stem-changing Verbs

Actividad 4 **En singular.** Change the subjects of the following sentences from **nosotros** to **yo** and make all other necessary changes.

1. Podemos ir a la fiesta. ______________________________
2. Dormimos ocho horas todas las noches. ______________________________
3. No servimos vino. ______________________________
4. Nos divertimos mucho. ______________________________
5. Nos acostamos temprano. ______________________________
6. Jugamos al fútbol. ______________________________

Nombre ______________________________ Sección ________________ Fecha ______________

Actividad 5 **Verbos.** Complete the following sentences by selecting a logical verb and writing the appropriate form.

1. María no ____________________ venir hoy. (poder, entender)
2. Los profesores siempre ____________________ las ventanas. (jugar, cerrar)
3. Carmen y yo ____________________ estudiar esta noche. (volver, preferir)
4. Marisel siempre ____________________ temprano. (dormirse, encontrar)
5. Yo no ____________________ francés. (entender, pedir)
6. ¿A qué hora ____________________ el concierto? (despertarse, empezar)
7. Juan ____________________ ir a bailar esta noche. (decir, pensar)
8. Pablo es camarero; ahora está ____________________ cerveza. (servir, comenzar)
9. Nosotros ____________________ a casa esta tarde. (volver, poder)
10. ¿Qué ____________________ hacer Uds.? (querer, dormir)
11. ____________________ Ricardo y Germán mañana? (despertar, venir)
12. Los niños están jugando al fútbol y están ____________________ mucho. (querer, divertirse)
13. Yo siempre ____________________ la verdad. (sentarse, decir)
14. ¿Cuándo ____________________ Ud. las clases? (comenzar, servir)
15. Ellos dicen que ____________________ ir. (decir, querer)

Actividad 6 **Preguntas.** Answer the following questions about your life in complete sentences.

1. ¿A qué hora empiezan tus clases los lunes? Empiezan mis clases 5:00pm los lunes.
2. ¿A qué hora te acuestas los domingos por la noche? me aquesto 7:00pm losdomingos por la noche.
3. ¿Con quién almuerzas durante la semana? Almuerzo 12:00pm durante la semana.
4. ¿Dónde almuerzan Uds.? Almuerzan en la cafeteria.
5. ¿Puedes estudiar por la tarde o tienes que trabajar? Tengo en la enfermer
6. ¿Prefieres estudiar por la tarde o por la noche? Prefiero estudiar por la tarde.
7. Generalmente, ¿cuántas horas duermes cada noche? duermo seis anoras cada noche.

Actividad 7 **Un email a Chile.** Here you have one page from an email that Teresa is writing to a friend in Chile. First read the entire page; then reread the letter and complete it with the appropriate forms of the verbs found to the left of each paragraph. Note: You may use verbs more than once.

Asunto: Hola

divertirse
entender
estar
querer
salir
ser

...y cómo están tus clases? ¿Tienes mucho trabajo? Tengo unos amigos fantásticos. Una se llama Diana; (1)__________ de los Estados Unidos, pero (2)__________ en España estudiando literatura. Habla y (3)__________ español como tú y yo porque su familia (4)__________ de origen mexicano. Yo (5)__________ mucho cuando (6)__________ con ella porque siempre pasa algo interesante. Nosotras (7)__________ ir a Barcelona el fin de semana que viene y después irnos a Sitges para (8)__________ en la playa.

encontrar
poder
ponerse
saber
ser

Tengo otra amiga que a ti te gustaría. Se llama Marisel; (9)__________ de Venezuela. Tiene ropa, ropa y más ropa. Siempre (10)__________ ropa muy moderna. Yo siempre tengo problemas con la ropa; voy a muchas tiendas, pero no (11)__________ cosas bonitas. (12)__________ que no soy fea, pero no hay ropa para mí. En cambio, Marisel siempre (13)__________ encontrar algo que es perfecto para ella.

conocer
pensar
poder
querer
vivir

Si vienes a España, vas a (14)__________ a dos chicos muy simpáticos. (15)__________ en un apartamento y si tú (16)__________, (17)__________ vivir con ellos. Debes (18)__________ en venir porque te gustaría y tienes que...

Actividad 8 **Dos conversaciones.** Complete the following conversations with verbs from the lists provided. Follow this procedure: first, read one conversation; then go back, select the verbs, and fill in the blanks with the appropriate forms; when finished, reread the conversations and check to see that all the verbs agree with their subjects. Note: You may use verbs more than once.

1. Una conversación por teléfono (**divertirse, empezar, mirar, preferir, querer, saber, volver**)

—¡Aló!

—¿Jesús?

—Sí.

—Habla Rafael. Carmen y yo ______________________ ver la película de Ron Howard. ¿Quieres ir?

—¿A qué hora ______________________ la película?

—No ______________________.

—¿Por qué no ______________________ en el periódico?

—Buena idea... Es a las siete y cuarto en el Cine Rex.

—¿______________________ Uds. comer un sándwich antes?

—Claro. Siempre tengo hambre. Hoy Carmen ______________________ a casa a las cinco. ¿Dónde ______________________ comer tú?

—______________________ la comida de la Perla Asturiana porque es barata y es un lugar bonito.

—Buena idea; yo siempre ______________________ en esa cafetería porque los camareros son muy cómicos.

2. Una conversación con el médico (**acostarse, despertarse, dormir, dormirse, entender**)

—Normalmente, ¿a qué hora ______________________ Ud. por la noche?

—A la una y media.

—¡Qué tarde! ¿Y a qué hora ______________________?

—______________________ a las siete.

—¡Cinco horas y media! ¿No ______________________ Ud. en la oficina?

—No, pero yo ______________________ la siesta todos los días.

—Ah, ahora ______________________. En mi casa, nosotros también ______________________ la siesta.

Actividad 9 **El detective.** The detective is still watching the woman. Today is very boring because the woman isn't leaving her apartment and the detective has to watch everything through the windows. Write what the detective says into his microphone, including the time and the activity in progress. Use the verb **estar** + *present participle* (**-ando, -iendo**) to describe the activity in progress.

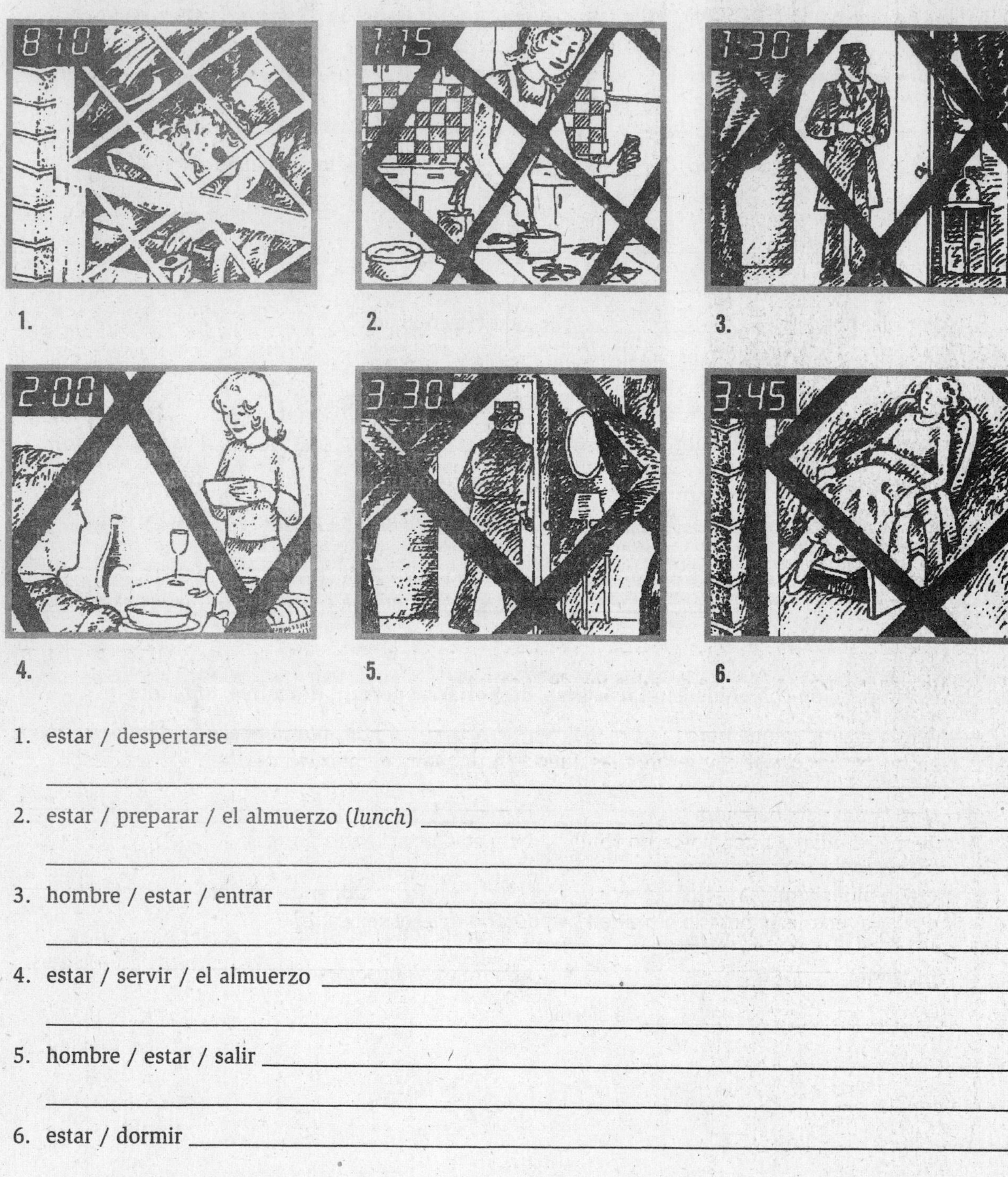

1. estar / despertarse ______________________________

____

2. estar / preparar / el almuerzo (*lunch*) ______________________________

____

3. hombre / estar / entrar ______________________________

____

4. estar / servir / el almuerzo ______________________________

____

5. hombre / estar / salir ______________________________

____

6. estar / dormir ______________________________

____

Nombre ______________________ Sección ______________ Fecha ____________

Un poco de todo

Actividad 10 **El horario de Pilar.** Pilar is a first-year student of philosophy. Look at her schedule (**horario**) and then answer the questions that follow.

	lunes	martes	miércoles	jueves	viernes
9:00–9:50	Antropología I	La herencia socrática	Antropología I	La herencia socrática	
10:05–11:05	Filosofía de la naturaleza	Teorías científicas de la cultura	Filosofía de la naturaleza	Teorías científicas de la cultura	Filosofía de la naturaleza
11:20–12:10	Metafísica I		Metafísica I		
12:25–1:25		Filosofía de la religión		Filosofía de la religión	
1:40–2:30	Fenomenología de la religión	Nihilismo y metafísica	Fenomenología de la religión	Nihilismo y metafísica	Fenomenología de la religión

1. ¿A qué hora empieza la clase de Antropología I los lunes y los miércoles?

____

2. ¿A qué hora puede tomar un café en la cafetería los martes?

____

3. ¿A qué hora termina la clase de Filosofía de la religión?

____

4. Normalmente las clases empiezan a las nueve. ¿A qué hora empiezan sus clases los viernes?

____

5. ¿Prefieren estudiar Antropología I o Nihilismo y metafísica tú y tus amigos?

____

6. ¿Te gustaría tener este horario o prefieres tu horario de este semestre?

____

Vocabulario esencial II

Los colores

Actividad 11 **Asociaciones.** Write the color or colors that you associate with each of the following things.

➤ las plantas ***verde***

1. el sol ______________________
2. los dientes ______________________
3. el océano Atlántico ______________________
4. el elefante Dumbo ______________________
5. el chocolate ______________________
6. la ecología ______________________
7. la bandera (*flag*) de Canadá ______________________
8. Tropicana, el pelo de Donald Trump y Sunkist ______________________
9. las bananas ______________________
10. la bandera de los Estados Unidos ______________________
11. el jugo Welch's ______________________

La ropa y los materiales (clothes and materials)

Actividad 12 **La ropa.** Identify the clothing items in this drawing. Include the definite article in your response.

1. ______________
2. ______________
3. ______________ 
4. ______________
5. ______________
6. ______________
7. ______________
8. ______________
9. ______________
10. ______________

Nombre ______________________ Sección ______________ Fecha ____________

Actividad 13 **En orden lógico.** Put the following words in logical order to form sentences. Make all necessary changes.

1. tener / suéter / ella / de / azul / lana / mi ______________________
2. camisas / el / para / comprar / yo / verano / ir a / algodón / de ______________________
3. gustar / rojo / me / pantalones / tus ______________________
4. yo / los / probarse / zapatos / alto / de / tacón / querer / negro ______________________

Actividad 14 **La importación.** Answer the following questions in complete sentences based on the clothes you are wearing.

1. ¿De dónde es tu camisa? ______________________
2. ¿De qué material es? ______________________
3. ¿Son de los Estados Unidos tus pantalones favoritos? ______________________
4. ¿De dónde son tus zapatos? ______________________
5. ¿Son de cuero? ______________________

Actividad 15 **Descripción.** Look at the accompanying drawing and describe what the people in it are wearing. Use complete sentences and be specific. Include information about colors and fabrics.

Actividad 16 **Tu ropa.** Using complete sentences, describe what you normally wear to class.

____

____

____

____

Gramática para la comunicación II

Indicating Purpose, Destination, and Duration: *Para* and *por*

Actividad 17 ***Por* o *para*.** Complete the following sentences with **por** or **para**.

1. La blusa es ________________ mi madre porque mañana es su cumpleaños.
2. Salimos el sábado ________________ Lima.
3. Voy a vivir en la universidad ________________ dos años más.
4. Álvaro estudia ________________ ser abogado.
5. Ahora Carlos trabaja los sábados ________________ la noche.
6. Vamos a Costa Rica ________________ dos semanas.
7. No me gusta ser camarero pero trabajo ________________ poder vestirme bien.
8. Tenemos que leer la novela ________________ mañana.
9. Mi amigo estudia ________________ ser médico.
10. Esta noche tengo que estudiar ________________ un mínimo de seis horas.
11. ¿Vas ________________ tu casa ahora?
12. Durante los veranos yo trabajo ________________ un banco en mi pueblo.

Indicating the Location of a Person, Thing, or Event: *Estar en* and *ser en*

Actividad 18 **¿Dónde es o dónde está?** Complete each sentence with the appropriate form of **ser** or **estar**.

1. Mi padre ________________ en Acapulco este fin de semana.
2. La fiesta ________________ en casa de Paco.
3. ¿Dónde ________________ los niños?
4. El concierto de Ricardo Arjona ________________ en el estadio.
5. Los libros ________________ en la biblioteca.
6. ¿Dónde ________________ la exhibición de Picasso?

Continued on next page →

Nombre ______________________ Sección ______________ Fecha ____________

7. Muchos cuadros de Picasso ___son___ en Barcelona en el Museo Picasso.
8. El presidente ___esta___ en la Casa Blanca.
9. La bufanda que quieres ___esta___ en Bloomingdale's.

Actividad 19 **Los viajes.** All of the following people are currently traveling. Say where they are from and imagine where they are right now. Use complete sentences.

1. Salma Hayek ___Ella esta en Espana___
2. Denzel Washington ___El esta actor.___
3. Tus padres ___son de milwaukee___
4. Enrique Iglesias ___es de es___

Un poco de todo

Actividad 20 ***Ser* o *estar*.** Complete the following sentences with the appropriate form of **ser** or **estar.** Don't forget the other uses of **ser** and **estar** you've studied. See **Capítulo 3** if needed.

1. Tu camisa ___es___ de algodón, ¿no?
2. Mis padres ___estan___ en Paraguay.
3. ¿De dónde ___son___ tus zapatos?
4. ¿Dónde ___estan___ tus zapatos?
5. El concierto ___es___ en el Teatro Colón.
6. Tus libros ___estas___ en la biblioteca.
7. ¿Dónde ___esta___ la fiesta?
8. ¿Dónde ___esta___ Daniel?
9. Daniel ___esta___ de Cuba, ¿no?
10. ¿___Son___ de plástico o de vidrio tus gafas de sol?

Actividad 21 **¿Dónde están?** Read the following miniconversations and complete the sentences with an appropriate verb. Afterward, tell where each conversation is taking place.

1. —¿A qué hora ______________ la película, por favor?

   —A las nueve y cuarto.

   ¿Dónde están? ______________________________

2. —¿Cuánto ______________ la habitación?

   —52 euros.

   —¿Tiene dos camas o una cama?

   —Dos.

   ¿Dónde están? ______________________________

3. —¿Qué hora es?

   — ______________ las dos y media.

   —¿Siempre ______________ Ud. aquí?

   —Sí, es un lugar excelente para pedir hamburguesas vegetarianas.

   ¿Dónde están? ______________________________

4. —¿Aló?

   —Hola, Roberto. ______________ hablar con tu padre.

   —Está ______________ en el sofá.

   —Bueno. Voy a llamar más tarde.

   ¿Dónde están Roberto y su padre? ______________

Actividad 22 **¡A comprar!** Complete the following conversation between a store clerk and a customer who is looking for a gift for his girlfriend.

CLIENTE Buenos días.

VENDEDORA ¿En qué ______________ servirle?

CLIENTE Me gustaría ver una blusa.

VENDEDORA ¿ ______________ quién?

CLIENTE ______________ mi novia porque es su cumpleaños. Es que ella ______________ Ecuador y yo salgo ______________ Quito mañana.

VENDEDORA Muy ______________. ¿De qué color?

CLIENTE ______________, ______________ o ______________.

VENDEDORA Aquí tiene tres blusas.

Continued on next page →

CLIENTE ¿Son de ______________________?

VENDEDORA Esta es de algodón, ______________________ las otras ______________________ seda.

CLIENTE No, no quiero una de algodón, ______________________ una blusa de seda.

VENDEDORA ¿____?

CLIENTE Creo que es 36.

VENDEDORA Bien, 36. Aquí están. Son muy ______________________.

CLIENTE ¡Ay! Estas sí. Me gustan mucho.

VENDEDORA Y ______________________ solamente 60 euros. ¿Cuál quiere?

CLIENTE Quiero la blusa ______________________.

VENDEDORA Es un color muy bonito.

CLIENTE También necesito una corbata ______________________ mí.

VENDEDORA ¿Con rayas o de un solo color? ¿De qué material?

CLIENTE Todas mis corbatas son de ______________________. Y tengo muchas de rayas. Creo que quiero una azul.

VENDEDORA Aquí hay ______________________ que ______________________ muy elegante.

CLIENTE Perfecto.

VENDEDORA ¿Cómo va a ______________________?

CLIENTE Con la tarjeta Visa.

VENDEDORA Si la talla no le queda ______________________ a su novia, yo siempre estoy aquí ______________________ las tardes.

CLIENTE Muchas gracias.

VENDEDORA De nada y buen viaje.

Lectura

Estrategia de lectura: Activating Background Knowledge

Predicting helps activate background knowledge, which aids you in forming hypotheses before you read. As you read, you confirm or reject these hypotheses based on the information given. As you reject them, you form new ones and the process of deciphering written material continues. Before reading an article about festivals in Latin America, you will be asked some questions to activate your background knowledge.

Actividad 23 **¿Qué sabes?** Before reading the article, answer these questions to activate your background knowledge about the Hispanic celebrations you read about in **Capítulo 5** of your textbook.

1. En el libro de texto, hay una lectura que explica las Fallas de Valencia, España, las Posadas en México y el Carnaval en Venezuela. Estos festivales ________.
   a. celebran un día o evento importante para los católicos
   b. celebran un evento importante en la historia de su país
   c. son para recordar grupos especiales (por ejemplo: los trabajadores, los amantes, las madres, etc.)
2. En las celebraciones de las Fallas, las Posadas y Carnaval, la gente ________. Marca todas las respuestas posibles.
   a. se pone ropa especial
   b. sale a la calle (*street*) para celebrar
   c. se queda en casa con su familia todos los días
   d. celebra con otras personas

Actividad 24 **Palabras desconocidas.** While reading, try to discern from context what the following words mean.

1. Inti Raymi
   extranjeros (línea 17) ______________________________
   siglo (línea 17) ______________________________
2. El día de Santiago apóstol
   estatua (línea 40) ______________________________
   la bomba (línea 43) ______________________________
   triunfan (línea 43) ______________________________

Nombre ______________________ Sección ______________ Fecha ___________

Celebraciones del mundo hispano

Inti Raymi

Festival de Inti Raymi en las ruinas de Saqsaywaman

Francisco Pizarro conquista a los incas y poco después, en 1572, el festival Inti Raymi deja de existir por orden de la iglesia católica por ser una celebración pagana. En el año 1944, los habitantes de Cuzco, muchos de ellos descendientes de los incas, empiezan a celebrar Inti Raymi otra vez. Inti Raymi es el festival del sol porque marca el solsticio de invierno. La fiesta dura una semana y marca el final de un año y el principio de otro en el calendario inca.

El 24 de junio los eventos empiezan en la ciudad de Cuzco con una procesión de dos kilómetros. Va hasta las ruinas de Saqsaywaman donde las personas representan una antigua ceremonia incaica en que el jefe de los incas honra a su dios, el Sol. Participan cientos de personas que llevan ropa tradicional mientras peruanos de todo el país y unos 100.000 turistas extranjeros van para mirar la ceremonia. Como en el siglo XVI, el líder de los incas, que se llama el Sapa Inca, habla y también hablan tres personas vestidas de animales: una serpiente, un puma y un cóndor. Los animales representan el mundo que existe debajo de la tierra, la tierra y el mundo de los dioses respectivamente. Todo es igual excepto que hoy día no sacrifican una llama, solo representan esta antigua tradición. Para leer más, haz clic **aquí.**

El día de Santiago[1] apóstol

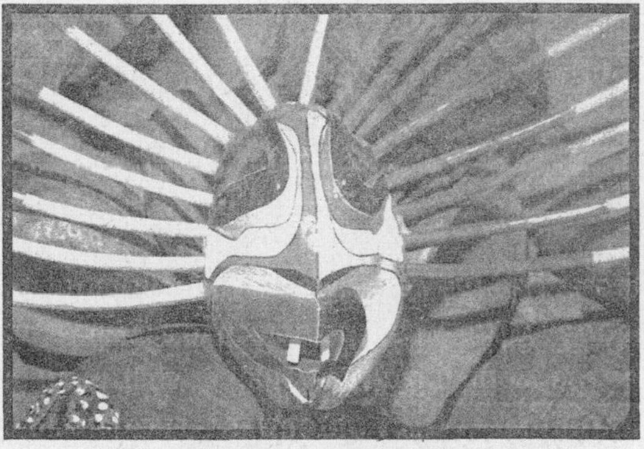

Máscara de un vejigante

La gente de Loíza Aldea, Puerto Rico, es principalmente de ascendencia africana. En este pueblo se puede ver el sincretismo religioso y cultural de los ritos paganos combinados con los ritos cristianos cuando celebran el día de Santiago apóstol el 25 de julio. En esta fiesta la gente le pide[2] favores a Santiago como buena salud, mucho dinero y matrimonio. Los protagonistas de la fiesta son los vejigantes (símbolo de la cultura africana) y los caballeros (representantes de la tradición católica española). Los vejigantes representan demonios y los caballeros representan a los caballeros españoles que luchan[3], igual que el apóstol Santiago, contra los demonios. Los vejigantes se visten con ropa de colores brillantes y en la cara llevan máscaras grotescas de coco, una fruta típica de la región. Los niños tienen miedo de los vejigantes. La fiesta, a finales de julio, dura más o menos una semana, cada día la gente saca una estatua diferente de la iglesia: una es el Santiago de los hombres, otra el Santiago de las mujeres y la tercera es el Santiago de los niños. Se llaman Santiagón, Santiago y Santiaguito respectivamente. Se hacen desfiles[4] por las calles donde se puede escuchar el ritmo de la bomba, música tradicional de influencia africana. Al final, triunfan los caballeros y pierden los vejigantes así que el bien gana contra el mal. Para leer más, haz clic **aquí.**

---

[1]*Santiago = Saint James, known for leading the Christians in the reconquest of Spain from the invading Moors in the 8th century.* [2]*ask for* [3]*fight* [4]*parades*

Actividad 25 **¿Entendiste?** After reading the articles, answer the following questions.

Inti Raymi

1. ¿De quiénes son descendientes las personas de Cuzco? ______________________

2. ¿Dónde es la parte más importante de la celebración de Inti Raymi? ______________________

3. ¿La fiesta ocurre durante los días más cortos o más largos del año? ______________________

4. ¿A quién honra el Sapa Inca durante el festival? ______________________

El día de Santiago apóstol

1. ¿Cuál es el origen de la mayoría de la gente de Loíza Aldea? ______________________

2. ¿Qué combina la celebración de Santiago apóstol? ______________________

3. ¿Quiénes representan el mal, los vejigantes o los caballeros? ______________________

4. ¿Qué ropa llevan los vejigantes? ¿Qué llevan en la cara? ______________________

5. ¿Qué tipo de música tocan en los desfiles y cuál es el origen de esa música? ______________________

6. Al final, ¿quiénes ganan? ______________________

Nombre ______________________ Sección ______________ Fecha __________

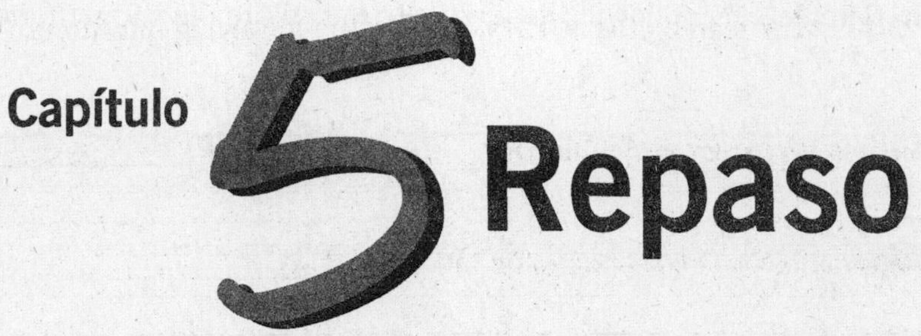

Capítulo 5 Repaso

Future, Present, and Immediate Past

You have learned to talk about obligations and plans, to state preferences, to say what you do every day, and to say what you are doing right now. You have also learned to state what has just happened.

Future obligations and plans:

Esta noche tengo que acostarme temprano.
Esta noche debo estudiar.
Esta noche voy a estudiar.
¿Cuándo vienes?
Pienso estudiar economía.
No puedo ir.

Preferences:

Me gustaría salir con mis amigos.
Me gusta comer en restaurantes e ir al cine.
Quiero ir contigo.
Prefiero la blusa roja.

What you do every day:

Yo me levanto temprano.
Vuelvo a casa tarde.
Voy al trabajo.
Miro la televisión.
Como con mis amigos.
Me acuesto temprano.

What you are doing right now:

Estoy leyendo.
Estoy estudiando.
Estoy haciendo la tarea.

What you just did:

Acabo de hablar con mi jefe.

Actividad 1 **Un email.** Complete the following email to a friend. Write the correct form of the indicated verbs in the blanks.

Asunto: Saludos

	Querida Mariana:
estar	¿Cómo ______________? Yo bien. En este momento
estar	______________ escuchando un disco compacto de Marc
gustar	Anthony. Me ______________ mucho, ¿y a ti? Un día me
gustar	______________ ver uno de sus conciertos. Tú
deber, comprar	______________ ______________ su nuevo CD porque
ser	______________ excelente.
ser	Aquí con el trabajo, todos los días ______________
levantarse, ducharse	iguales. ______________ temprano, ______________,
vestirse, tomar	______________ y ______________ un café en una
	cafetería cerca del trabajo. Este sábado no voy a
levantarse	______________ hasta las doce.
buscar	Tengo que ______________ un trabajo nuevo. De
gustar	verdad, no me ______________ mi jefe (*boss*). Además
querer	______________ vivir en Caracas para estar cerca de mis
gustar	padres. Me ______________ encontrar un trabajo de
acabar	profesora en una escuela. ______________ de leer en
necesitar	el periódico que ______________ profesores en una
	escuela bilingüe.
ser, salir	¿Cómo ______________ tu vida? ¿______________ con
ir, hacer	Tomás? ¿Qué ______________ a ______________ tú para las
gustar	vacaciones de Navidad? Me ______________ ir a una isla
tener	del Caribe, pero no ______________ dinero.
ir, venir	Mis padres ______________ a ______________ aquí para
ir, divertirse	Navidad. Nosotros ______________ a ______________
venir	mucho. ¿Por qué no ______________ tú? Un fuerte abrazo
	de tu amiga,
	Raquel

Nombre ____________________ Sección ____________ Fecha __________

Ayer y hoy

Vocabulario esencial I

Los números del cien al millón

Actividad 1 **Los números.** Write out the following numbers. Remember that in Spanish a period is used instead of a comma when writing large numbers.

a. 564 ____________________

b. 1.015 ____________________

c. 2.973 ____________________

d. 4.743.010 ____________________

Actividad 2 **Una serie de números.** Write the number that fits logically in each series.

1. doscientos, trescientos, cuatrocientos, ____________________
2. ochocientos, ____________________, seiscientos
3. cuatro millones, tres millones, dos millones, ____________________
4. ____________________, doscientos, trescientos, cuatrocientos
5. trescientos, seiscientos, ____________________
6. cuatro mil, tres mil, dos mil, ____________________
7. doscientos, trescientos, ____________________

Preposiciones de lugar

Actividad 3 **¿Dónde están?** In the first blank, write **C** (**cierto**) if the statement is true and **F** (**falso**) if the statement is false. Correct the false statements by writing the correct preposition (including the word **de** when needed) in the second space. All questions are based on the following configuration of letters.

		LH	
AB			I
C	D	EFG	J

Continued on next page →

	C/F	Preposición
1. La ce está debajo de la a.	____	________
2. La efe está encima de la e y la ge.	____	________
3. La ele está cerca de la be.	____	________
4. La i está entre la ele y la jota.	____	________
5. La ge está a la izquierda de la efe.	____	________
6. La jota está debajo de la i.	____	________
7. La be está cerca de la a.	____	________
8. La e está a la derecha de la efe.	____	________
9. La ge está al lado de la efe.	____	________
10. La ele está encima de la i.	____	________

Actividad 4 **¿Dónde está?** Using the accompanying drawing and different prepositions of location, write six sentences that describe where things are in Ricardo's bedroom.

➤ ***El equipo de audio esta al lado de la silla.***

1. ______________________________
2. ______________________________
3. ______________________________
4. ______________________________
5. ______________________________
6. ______________________________

Nombre ______________________ Sección ______________ Fecha __________

Gramática para la comunicación I

Talking about the Past: The Preterit

Actividad 5 **El pasado.** Complete the following sentences by selecting a logical verb and writing the appropriate preterit form.

1. Ayer yo ______________ con el Sr. Martínez. (hablar, costar)
2. Anoche nosotros no ______________ cerveza. (beber, comer)
3. Esta mañana Pepe ______________ al médico. (empezar, ir)
4. ¿Qué ______________ Ramón ayer? (hacer, vivir)
5. Anoche Marcos y Luis ______________ cinco kilómetros. (llevar, correr)
6. El verano pasado yo ______________ a Buenos Aires. (despertarse, ir)
7. Yo ______________ un buen restaurante, no ______________ uno y al final ______________ en una cafetería. (buscar, nadar) (encontrar, pagar) (correr, comer)
8. Guillermo, ¿______________ anoche con Mariana? (bailar, entender)
9. ¿______________ Ud. mi email? (vivir, recibir)
10. Tú ______________ la composición, ¿no? (escuchar, escribir)
11. Ayer yo ______________ 25 pesos por una camisa. (pagar, salir)
12. Ellos ______________ una tortilla de patatas. (hacer, beber)
13. Después del accidente, el niño ______________. (llorar, conocer)
14. Anoche yo ______________ a estudiar a las siete. (asistir, empezar)
15. ¿A qué hora ______________ la película? (pensar, terminar)

Actividad 6 **¿Qué hicieron?** Answer the following questions about you and your friends in complete sentences.

1. ¿Adónde fueron Uds. el sábado pasado? ______________
2. ¿A qué hora volvieron Uds. anoche? ______________
3. ¿Recibió un amigo un email de tu madre? ______________
4. ¿Visitaste a tus padres el mes pasado? ______________
5. ¿Pagaste tú la última vez que saliste con un/a chico/a? ______________
6. ¿Tomaste el autobús esta mañana para ir a la universidad? ______________
7. ¿Fuiste a una fiesta la semana pasada? ______________

Continued on next page →

8. ¿Quién compró Coca-Cola y papas fritas para la fiesta?

____

9. ¿Aprendieron Uds. mucho ayer en clase?

____

10. ¿Escribieron Uds. la composición para la clase de español?

____

11. ¿Quién no asistió a la clase de español esta semana?

____

Actividad 7 **¿Infinitivo o no?** Complete the following sentences with the appropriate form of the indicated verbs (present, preterit, infinitive) and add the preposition a if necessary.

1. Ayer nosotros ______________ y ______________. (cantar, bailar)
2. Ayer Margarita ______________ la clase de biología. (asistir)
3. Los músicos van a ______________ tocar a las ocho. (empezar)
4. Necesito ______________; tengo hambre. (comer)
5. Todos los días yo ______________ cuatro horas. (estudiar)
6. Debes ______________ más. (estudiar)
7. Me gusta ______________ en el invierno. (esquiar)
8. Ayer yo ______________ la piscina, pero no ______________. (ir, nadar)

Actividad 8 **Un día horrible.** Complete this conversation between two friends. First, read the entire conversation. Then, fill in the missing words by selecting verbs from the list and writing them in the appropriate forms. Note: You may use verbs more than once.

comer	hacer	perder	ser
dejar	ir	recibir	ver
encontrar	llegar	sacar	volver
escribir	pagar		

—Ayer ______________ un día increíble.

—¿Qué ______________ Uds.?

—______________ a ver una película. Después ______________ algo en un restaurante.

—¿Y?

—Qué idiota soy. Yo ______________ el dinero en el cine. ¡Qué vergüenza! Por eso María ______________ su reloj en el restaurante con un camarero. El camarero ______________ su nombre en un papel y guardó (*put away*) el reloj. ¡Un Rolex! Y

Continued on next page →

nosotros ______________________ al cine. Por fin, yo ______________________ el dinero.

—¡Huy! Gracias a Dios.

—No termina la historia.

—(Nosotros) ______________________ al restaurante y no ______________________ al camarero.

—¿Qué ______________________ Uds. entonces?

—Por fin, el camarero ______________________ y María ______________________ su reloj. Yo ______________________ el dinero de mi cartera (*wallet*) y ______________________ los 160 pesos.

Actividad 9 **¿Cuándo fue la última vez que...?** Explain when was the last time that you did the following things. The first one has been done as an example.

1. ir al médico	ayer
2. visitar a tus padres	anteayer
3. hablar por teléfono con tus abuelos	hace dos/tres días
4. comer en un restaurante	la semana pasada
5. levantarte tarde	hace dos/tres semanas
6. ir al dentista	el mes pasado
7. hacer un viaje	hace dos/tres meses
8. volver a tu escuela secundaria	el año pasado
9. comprar un CD	hace dos años
10. ir a un concierto	

1. *Hace tres meses que fui al médico*
2. ______________________
3. ______________________
4. ______________________
5. ______________________
6. ______________________
7. ______________________
8. ______________________
9. ______________________
10. ______________________

Actividad 10 **Un email.** Write an email to a friend telling him/her what you did last weekend and with whom, as well as what you are going to do next week.

Asunto: Mi fin de semana

Querido/a ______________________ :

¿Qué tal? ¿Cómo está tu familia? Por aquí todo bien. El viernes pasado ____.

El sábado pasado ____.

El domingo pasado nosotros ____.

La semana que viene yo ____

Un abrazo,

(tu nombre)

Indicating Relationships: Prepositions and Prepositional Pronouns

Actividad 11 **Espacios en blanco.** Fill in the following blanks with the appropriate preposition or prepositional pronoun. Use only one word per blank.

1. ¿Este dinero es para ______________? ¡Gracias!
2. No puedo vivir ______________ ti. Eres fantástico.
3. Después ______________ comer en el restaurante, fuimos al cine.
4. Entre ______________ y ______________ vamos a escribir la composición.
5. ______________ del examen, fui a hablar con el profesor; por eso, contesté a las preguntas muy bien y saqué buena nota en el examen.
6. Javier no asiste ______________ muchas clases; por eso va a sacar malas notas.
7. Ahora comienzo ______________ entender tu pregunta.

Continued on next page →

8. ¿Quieres ir ______________________ al cine el viernes?
9. Antonio Banderas se casó ______________________ Melanie Griffith.
10. Estoy aburrida. ¿Por qué no salimos ______________________ aquí?
11. No quiero salir más ______________________. Eres un desastre.

Actividad 12 **La telenovela.** One of your friends is in South America and can not see her favorite soap opera. Complete the following summary for her of what happened during this week's episodes. First, read the entire summary. Then, complete the story with the appropriate prepositions or prepositional pronouns.

Maruja dejó a su esposo Felipe, y se va a casar ______________ Javier, el mecánico de la señora rica (entre ______________ y ______________, ella está loca porque, como tú sabes, Javier no es simpático). Entonces, Felipe decidió no ir más a Alcohólicos Anónimos y empezó ______________ beber otra vez. Él cree que no puede vivir ______________ ella. Felipe compró un regalo muy caro y en la tarjeta escribió, "Para ______________, con todo mi amor para siempre, tu Felipe". Después, ella habló ______________ Javier por teléfono sobre el regalo y él no dijo nada.

Pero más tarde ella fue a la casa de Javier, abrió la puerta y encontró a Javier ______________ otra mujer. Ella empezó a llorar y salió corriendo ______________ la casa de Felipe. Y así terminó el programa del viernes. Como me vas a llamar el martes, puedo hablar ______________ de qué ocurre el lunes.

Un poco de todo

Actividad 13 **¿Qué ocurrió?** Last night you went out to a restaurant and a club with some friends, including Carmen, Ramón's ex-girlfriend. Since Ramón couldn't go, he wants to know all the details of the evening. Read all of Ramón's questions first; then complete your part of the conversation.

RAMÓN ¿Carmen salió contigo anoche?
TÚ ____

RAMÓN ¿Quiénes más fueron?
TÚ ____

RAMÓN ¿Adónde fueron y qué hicieron?
TÚ ____

RAMÓN ¿Habló mucho Carmen con Andrés?
TÚ ____

RAMÓN ¿Qué más hizo con él?
TÚ ____

RAMÓN Bueno, ¿y tú qué?
TÚ ____

Vocabulario esencial II

La familia de Diana

Actividad 14 **La familia.** Complete the following sentences.

1. La hermana de mi madre es mi ______________________.
2. El padre de mi padre es mi ______________________.
3. Los hijos de mis padres son mis ______________________.
4. La hija de mi tío es mi ______________________.
5. Mi ______________________ es la hija de mi abuelo y la esposa de mi padre.
6. La esposa del hermano de mi madre es mi ______________________.
7. Mi ______________________ es el hijo de mis abuelos y el padre de mi primo.
8. Mi padre se casó por segunda vez; su nueva esposa es mi ______________________.
9. Los hijos del hijo de mi madre son mis ______________________.
10. Mis hermanos son los ______________________ de mis abuelos.
11. No es mi hermana pero es la nieta de mis abuelos; es mi ______________________.
12. Mi madre se casó con un hombre que tiene dos hijos. Esos hijos son los ______________________ de mi madre y son mis ______________________.

Actividad 15 **Mi familia. Parte A.** List five of your relatives. For each of these relatives, indicate his/her name, relationship to you, age, occupation, marital status (single, married, or divorced), any children he/she may have, and whether he/she is a favorite relative. Follow the format shown in the example.

➤ ***Betty:* abuela—74 años—jubilada** (retired)**—divorciada—4 hijos—mi abuela favorita**
***Clarence:* abuelo—69 años—pintor—casado (con Helen)—2 hijos**
Etc.

1. ____
____
2. ____
____
3. ____
____
4. ____
____
5. ____
____

Parte B. Use information from **Parte A** to write a short composition about a member of your family.

____

____

____

____

____

____

Gramática para la comunicación II

Using Indirect-Object Pronouns

Actividad 16 **Complementos indirectos.** Complete the following sentences with the appropriate indirect-object pronouns.

1. ¿________________ escribiste un email a tu hermano?
2. Ayer ________________ diste (a mí) el libro de cálculo.
3. A ti ________________ gusta esquiar.
4. Ayer ________________ mandé el regalo a ellos.
5. ¿________________ diste a Carlos y a mí el disco compacto?
6. ¿Qué ________________ regalaste a tus padres para su aniversario?
7. ¿________________ diste mi trabajo al profesor Galaraga?
8. Carlos ________________ explicó su problema, ¿no? Ahora entiendes por qué está tan triste.

Actividad 17 **Preguntas y respuestas.** Answer the following questions in the affirmative in complete sentences.

1. ¿Te dio dinero tu padre el fin de semana pasado?

   ____
2. ¿Le ofrecieron el trabajo a Carlos? ______________________________________

   ____
3. ¿Le dieron a Ud. el informe Pablo y Fernando? ______________________________

   ____
4. ¿Me vas a escribir? ____
5. ¿Les explicaron a Uds. la verdad? ____
6. ¿Me estás hablando? ____

Actividad 18 **¿Qué hiciste?** Your roommate is sick and asked you to do a few things. He/She still has a few more requests. Answer his/her questions, using indirect-object pronouns.

COMPAÑERO/A ¿Le mandaste a mi tía la carta que te di?

TÚ Sí, ______________________________

COMPAÑERO/A ¿Me compraste el champú y la pasta de dientes? ¿Cuánto te costaron?

TÚ Sí, ______________________________

____

COMPAÑERO/A ¿Le diste la composición al profesor de historia?

TÚ Sí, ______________________________

____

COMPAÑERO/A ¿Le dejaste la nota al profesor de literatura?

TÚ No, ______________________________

____

COMPAÑERO/A ¿Nos dio tarea la profesora de cálculo?

TÚ No, ______________________________

____

COMPAÑERO/A ¿Me buscaste el libro en la biblioteca?

TÚ Sí, ______________________________

____

COMPAÑERO/A ¿Les vas a decir a Adrián y a Pilar que no puedo ir a esquiar mañana?

TÚ Sí, ______________________________

____

COMPAÑERO/A ¿Esta noche me puedes comprar papel para la computadora?

TÚ No, ______________________________

____

Using Affirmative and Negative Words

Actividad 19 **Negativos.** Rewrite the following sentences in the negative. Use **nada, nadie,** or **nunca.**

1. Siempre estudio. ______________________________
2. Hago muchas cosas. ______________________________
3. Él sale con su novia. ______________________________
4. Voy al parque todos los días. ______________________________
5. Compró mucho. ______________________________

Nombre ______________________ Sección ______________ Fecha __________

Actividad 20 **La negación.** Using complete sentences, answer the following questions in the negative. Use **nada, nadie,** or **nunca.**

1. ¿Esquías todos los inviernos? ______________________
2. ¿Bailaste con alguien anoche? ______________________
3. ¿Quién fue a la fiesta? ______________________
4. ¿Qué le regalaste a tu madre para su cumpleaños? ______________________

   ____
5. ¿Siempre visitas a tus abuelos? ______________________
6. ¿Tiene Ud. 20 pesos? ______________________

Actividad 21 **Niño triste.** Complete the following paragraph with affirmative or negative words. Use **algo, alguien, siempre, nada, nadie,** and **nunca.**

Es el primer día de clases y Pablo está triste, requetetriste porque está en un país nuevo. No tiene amigos, y no juega con ______________ en el parque. No estudia ______________ porque no entiende ______________. ______________ habla en inglés con el y ______________ comprende sus problemas. No tiene ______________ que hacer y quiere volver a su país. La madre de Pablo no está preocupada porque ella sabe que él va a aprender a decir ______________ en el idioma pronto y que ______________ va a empezar a jugar con su hijo. Los niños ______________ hacen amigos nuevos y se adaptan a diferentes situaciones en poco tiempo.

Un poco de todo

Actividad 22 **La novia y los padres de él.** Manuel's girlfriend, Laura, spent an afternoon with his parents while he was at a convention. It was the first time they met her. Complete Laura's side of the conversation with Manuel where he finds out how things went.

MANUEL ¿Hicieron Uds. algo especial?

LAURA No, no hicimos ______________________

MANUEL ¿Adónde fueron?

LAURA ______________________

MANUEL ¿Conociste a alguien más de mi familia?

LAURA No, no ______________________

MANUEL ¿Mi madre te habló de mí?

LAURA Sí, ______________________

Continued on next page →

MANUEL ¿Hablaron de algo en especial?

LAURA No, no ______________________________, solo un poco de los políticos corruptos, de las películas de Gael García Bernal, de los nuevos escándalos de Hollywood. Como ves, nada en particular. Ah... y claro, para ellos tú eres muy especial.

MANUEL ¿Y te gustaron mis padres?

LAURA Sí, son muy ______________________________

Lectura

Estrategia de lectura: Skimming and Scanning

Skimming is a skill used for getting the gist of written materials. For example, you skim the contents of a newspaper, reading only the headlines and glancing at the photos to see which articles might interest you. Once you find an article of interest, you may then skim or scan it. Skimming means merely reading quickly to get the general message. Scanning means looking for specific details to answer questions that you already have in mind.

Actividad 23 **Lectura rápida.** Skim the article on page 101 to find out what the main topic is:

a. geography and peoples of South America

b. peoples of South America

c. geography of South America

Actividad 24 **Lectura enfocada.** Scan the following article to find the answers to these questions.

1. ¿Dónde está el Atacama y qué es? ______________________________
____

2. ¿Dónde están las montañas más altas de América? ______________________________
____

3. ¿Dónde encontró Darwin animales casi prehistóricos? ______________________________
____

4. ¿Son tristes o alegres las leyendas? ______________________________
____

Nombre ______________________ Sección ______________ Fecha ___________

SURAMÉRICA: UNA MARAVILLA

El volcán Osorno, Chile

La diversidad natural de Suramérica es extraordinaria. Cuando los españoles llegaron a fines del siglo XV, encontraron una tierra muy rica y variada, pero que les causó muchos problemas por su diversidad natural. No fue fácil explorar las tierras vírgenes del río Amazonas, el desierto de Atacama en Chile y los Andes cubiertos de nieve. Al llegar los conquistadores españoles a lo que hoy día es la frontera entre Argentina y Chile, vieron las montañas más altas de todo el continente americano y, cuando las cruzaron, **llegaron** al océano Pacífico. También encontraron el delta del Río de la Plata, entre Uruguay y Argentina, que les ofreció lugares ideales para construir las ciudades de Buenos Aires, La Plata y Montevideo. El delta les dio acceso al interior por el río y al continente europeo por el océano Atlántico: Un sitio perfecto para los comerciantes.

En 1492, los españoles encontraron un continente ya habitado por los indígenas y aprendieron de ellos muchas cosas. Así, siguiendo el ejemplo de los indígenas, la llama en la cordillera andina y la canoa en los ríos Orinoco, Amazonas y Paraná resultaron ser para ellos medios de transporte mucho mejores que los caballos[1] y las caravelas[2] que trajeron de España. Pronto los españoles aprendieron a moverse por esas tierras, explorando diferentes lugares y conociendo la vida y costumbres de los habitantes. Los indígenas **les** contaron leyendas regionales. Como muchas otras leyendas, **estas** explican el origen de lugares geográficos y casi siempre aparecen en ellas seres humanos y dioses. Por ejemplo, las leyendas dicen que los dioses **se enfadaron** y crearon las cataratas del Iguazú entre Argentina y Brasil y los Cuernos del Paine, montañas en Chile. En el caso de Iguazú, un dios se enfadó tanto que mató a dos amantes con un torrente de agua, y en el otro, el dios se enfadó con dos guerreros y con ellos formó montañas. Estas leyendas pasaron oralmente de generación en generación y hoy día forman parte del folclore suramericano.

Las cataratas del Iguazú, Argentina

En el siglo XXI la diversidad natural de Suramérica todavía nos ofrece mucha belleza y recursos naturales. Las cataratas del Iguazú son majestuosas y le dan electricidad a un área muy extensa. Los Cuernos del Paine forman parte de un parque nacional que es magnífico para hacer ecoturismo. Las islas Galápagos, que con sus animales casi prehistóricos **le** dieron a Darwin la oportunidad de investigar su teoría de la evolución, son un tesoro de la naturaleza. Suramérica es también rica en minerales como el cobre[3] de Chile, el petróleo de Venezuela, el estaño[4] de Bolivia y el carbón de Colombia. Además, la misma tierra que nos **dio** la papa, todavía es rica en vegetación y exporta flores, bananas, café y muchos otros productos.

Los españoles llegaron a América con la idea de conquistar, explorar y llevar mucho oro[5] a España, pero no pensaron en la importancia de las riquezas naturales del Nuevo Mundo. Su llegada empezó un nuevo capítulo en la historia suramericana. Ahora, en el siglo XXI, estamos empezando a escribir otro capítulo, pero debemos ser conscientes y no destruir la belleza y las riquezas naturales que forman esa tierra tan maravillosa.

---

[1]*horses* [2]*ships, caravels* [3]*copper* [4]*tin* [5]*gold*

Actividad 25 **Los detalles.** Answer the following questions based on the reading.

1. ¿Cuál es el sujeto del verbo **llegaron** en el párrafo 1? ______________________
2. ¿Por qué fue un lugar ideal el Río de la Plata para construir ciudades? ______________________
____
3. ¿Qué animal usaron los indígenas para transportar cosas en la zona andina? ______________________
4. ¿A quiénes se refiere **les** en el párrafo 2? ______________________
5. ¿A qué se refiere **estas** en el párrafo 2? ______________________
6. ¿Cuál es el sujeto del verbo **se enfadaron** en el párrafo 2? ______________________
7. ¿Cuál es un sinónimo de **se enfadaron**? ______________________
8. ¿A quién se refiere **le** en el párrafo 3? ______________________
9. ¿Cuál es el sujeto de **dio** en el párrafo 3? ______________________
10. ¿Hoy día qué productos exporta Suramérica? ______________________
____
11. ¿De qué debemos ser conscientes en el siglo XXI? ______________________
____

Nombre ______________________ Sección ______________ Fecha ____________

Capítulo 7 Los viajes

Vocabulario esencial I

El teléfono

Actividad 1 **Hablando por teléfono.** Match the sentences in Column A with the logical responses from Column B.

A	B
1. _____ ¿Aló?	a. Tiene Ud. el número equivocado.
2. _____ ¿De parte de quién?	b. ¿Para hablar con quién?
3. _____ ¿Hablo con el 233-44-54?	c. Buenos días, ¿está Tomás?
4. _____ Operadora internacional, buenos días.	d. ¿Por qué? ¿Tienes la batería baja?
5. _____ Tenemos que hablar rápido.	e. Quisiera el número del cine Rex, en la calle Luna.
6. _____ Información, buenos días.	f. Quisiera hacer una llamada a Panamá.
7. _____ No estamos en casa. Puede dejar un mensaje después del tono.	g. No me gusta hablar con máquinas. Te veo esta tarde.
8. _____ Lo siento, pero Carlos no está.	h. ¿Le puede decir que llamó Héctor?
	i. Habla Félix.

Actividad 2 **Número equivocado.** Complete the following conversations that Camila has as she tries to reach her friend Imelda by telephone.

1. SEÑORA ¿Aló?
   CAMILA ¿______________________ Imelda?
   SEÑORA No, ______________________________________.
   CAMILA ¿No es el 4-49-00-35?
   SEÑORA Sí, pero ______________________________________.

Continued on next page →

2. OPERADORA Información.

CAMILA _______________________________ Imelda García Arias.

OPERADORA El número es 8-34-88-75.

CAMILA _______________________________

3. SEÑOR ¿_______________________?

CAMILA ¿_______________________________?

SEÑOR Sí, ¿_______________________________?

CAMILA _______________________ Camila.

SEÑOR Un momento. Ahora viene.

En el hotel

Actividad 3 **¿Quién es o qué es?** Complete the following sentences with the logical words.

1. Una habitación para una persona es _______________________.
2. Una habitación para dos personas es _______________________.
3. La persona que limpia (*cleans*) el hotel es _______________________.
4. La persona que trabaja en recepción es _______________________.
5. Una habitación con desayuno y una comida es _______________________.
6. Una habitación con todas las comidas es _______________________.
7. El dinero extra que le das al botones es _______________________.

Actividad 4 **En el Hotel Meliá.** Complete the following conversation between a guest and a receptionist at the Hotel Meliá. First, read the entire conversation. Then, go back and complete it appropriately.

RECEPCIONISTA Buenos días. ¿_______________ puedo servirle?

CLIENTE Necesito una _______________________.

RECEPCIONISTA ¿Con una o dos camas?

CLIENTE Dos, por favor.

RECEPCIONISTA ¿_______________________________? Es más económico si no tiene.

CLIENTE Con baño.

RECEPCIONISTA ¿_______________________________?

CLIENTE Con media pensión.

RECEPCIONISTA Bien, una habitación doble con baño y media pensión.

CLIENTE ¿_______________________________?

RECEPCIONISTA 125 euros. ¿_______________________________?

CLIENTE Vamos a estar tres noches.

RECEPCIONISTA Bien. Su habitación es la 24.

Nombre ______________________ Sección ______________ Fecha ____________

Gramática para la comunicación I

Talking About the Past

Actividad 5 **Los verbos en el pasado.** Complete the following sentences with the appropriate preterit form of the indicated verbs.

1. ¿Dónde ______________ tú las cartas? (poner)
2. Ayer yo no ______________ ver a mi amigo. (poder)
3. ¿A qué hora ______________ anoche el concierto? (comenzar)
4. La semana pasada la policía ______________ la verdad. (saber)
5. Nosotros ______________ la cerveza. (traer)
6. ¿Por qué no ______________ los padres de Ramón? (venir)
7. La profesora ______________ las preguntas dos veces. (repetir)
8. Yo no ______________ tiempo para estudiar. (tener)
9. Martín ______________ el email que Paco le ______________ a Carmen. (leer, escribir)
10. Yo le ______________ a José el número de teléfono de Beatriz. (pedir)
11. Yo ______________ dormir, pero no ______________. (querer, poder)
12. La compañía ______________ unas oficinas nuevas en la calle Lope de Rueda. (construir)
13. Ellos no nos ______________ la verdad ayer. (decir)
14. ¿______________ tú que ______________ el padre de Raúl? (oír, morirse)
15. Anoche Gonzalo ______________ en su carro. (dormir)

Actividad 6 **La vida universitaria.** In complete sentences, answer the following survey questions from a student newspaper.

1. ¿Cuántas horas dormiste anoche? ______________
2. ¿Cuándo fue la última vez que mentiste? ______________
3. ¿Estudiaste mucho o poco para tu último examen? ______________
4. ¿Qué nota sacaste en tu último examen? ______________
5. ¿A cuántas fiestas fuiste el mes pasado? ______________
6. La última vez que saliste de la universidad por un fin de semana, ¿llevaste los libros? ______________

Continued on next page →

7. ¿Cuánto tiempo hace que leíste una novela para divertirte? ______________________________

____

8. ¿Comiste bien o comiste mal (papas fritas, Coca-Cola, etc.) anoche? ______________________

____

Actividad 7 **Las obligaciones.** In Column A of the accompanying chart, list three things you had to do and did do yesterday (**tuve que**). In Column B, list three things you had to do but refused to do (**no quise**). In Column C, list three things you have to do tomorrow (**tengo que**). Use complete sentences.

A	B	C

Expressing the Duration of an Action: *Hace que*

Actividad 8 **¿Presente o pretérito?** Answer the following questions in complete sentences, using either the present or the preterit.

1. ¿Cuánto tiempo hace que estudias español? ______________________________

____

2. ¿Cuánto tiempo hace que comiste? ______________________________

____

3. ¿Cuánto tiempo hace que viven tus padres en su casa? ______________________________

____

4. ¿Cuánto tiempo hace que asistes a esta universidad? ______________________________

____

5. ¿Cuánto tiempo hace que hablaste con tu madre? ______________________________

____

Nombre ______________________ Sección ______________ Fecha ____________

Un poco de todo

Actividad 9 **¿Cuánto tiempo hace que...?** Look at this portion of Mario Huidobro's résumé. Complete the questions with the appropriate forms of the verbs **trabajar, tocar, vender,** or **terminar.** Remember: Use **hace** + *time period* + *present* to refer to actions that started in the past and continue to the present; use **hace** + *time period* + *preterit* to refer to actions that happened in the past and do not continue to the present.

Guadalajara, de 1996 a 2000: estudiante universitario y recepcionista en el hotel Camino Real
Querétaro, de 2000 al presente: pianista profesional
Querétaro, de 2000 al presente: vendedor de computadoras para Dell

1. ¿Cuánto tiempo hace que Mario ______________ como recepcionista?
____
2. ¿Cuánto tiempo hace que Mario ______________ el piano profesionalmente?
____
3. ¿Cuánto tiempo hace que Mario ______________ sus estudios universitarios?
____
4. ¿Cuánto tiempo hace que Mario ______________ computadoras para Dell?
____

Vocabulario esencial II

Medios de transporte

Actividad 10 **El transporte.** Write the transportation-related word that you associate with each of the following words or groups of words. Include the appropriate definite article.

1. Amtrak ______________
2. Trek, Schwinn ______________
3. Volkswagen, Honda, Buick ______________
4. U-Haul, Ryder ______________
5. LAX, O'Hare, J.F.K., Logan ______________
6. Ford Explorer, Jeep Cherokee, Suburban ______________
7. BART (San Francisco), El (Chicago), T (Boston) ______________
8. Harley-Davidson, Kawasaki ______________
9. United, Aeroméxico, Jet Blue, Iberia, LACSA ______________
10. Titanic ______________
11. Greyhound ______________

Actividad 11 **Transporte en Barcelona.** Complete the following travel guide description about the modes of transportation in Barcelona.

Al aeropuerto de Barcelona llegan ______________________ de vuelos (*flights*) nacionales e internacionales. Como el aeropuerto está a diez kilómetros de la ciudad, se puede tomar un ______________________, pero hay un servicio de autobuses a la ciudad que cuesta menos. Como Barcelona está en la costa, también llegan ______________________ de Italia y de otras partes del Mediterráneo. Existen dos estaciones de ______________________; a muchas personas les gusta este medio rápido de transporte porque pueden dormir durante el viaje en una cama. Dentro de la ciudad el transporte público es muy bueno y cuesta poco: hay ______________________, ______________________ y, por supuesto, ______________________, que cuestan más. El ______________________ es el medio más rápido porque no importan los problemas de tráfico. Muchas personas prefieren conducir su ______________________, pero es difícil encontrar dónde dejarlo, especialmente en la parte vieja de la ciudad. Como en todas las ciudades grandes, hay pocos lugares para aparcar.

El pasaje y el aeropuerto

Actividad 12 **De viaje.** Complete the following sentences with the word being defined.

1. La hora en que llega el vuelo es la ______________________.
2. Si un avión llega tarde, llega con ______________________.
3. Si vas de Nueva York a Tegucigalpa y vuelves a Nueva York es un viaje de ______________________.
4. La hora en que sale el vuelo es la ______________________.
5. La persona que viaja es un ______________________.
6. Si vas de Nueva York a Tegucigalpa pero el avión va primero a Miami, el vuelo hace ______________________.
7. Si el vuelo no va a Miami (como en la pregunta anterior), es un vuelo ______________________.
8. La silla de un avión se llama ______________________.
9. Iberia, Lan Chile y Avianca son ______________________.
10. El equipaje que puedes llevar contigo en el avión es el ______________________.
11. El asiento que está entre el asiento de la ventanilla y el del pasillo es el ______________________.
12. La tarjeta que presentas para subir al avión es la tarjeta de ______________________.

Nombre ______________________ Sección ______________ Fecha ____________

Actividad 13 **Información.** Give or ask for flight information based on the accompanying arrival and departure boards from the international airport in Caracas. Use complete sentences.

Llegadas Internacionales				
Línea aérea	**Nº de vuelo**	**Procedencia**	**Hora de llegada**	**Comentarios**
Iberia	952	Lima	09:50	a tiempo
VIASA	354	Santo Domingo	10:29	11:05
LAN Chile	988	Santiago/Miami	12:45	a tiempo
Lacsa	904	México/N.Y.	14:00	14:35

Salidas Internacionales					
Línea aérea	**Nº de vuelo**	**Destino**	**Hora de salida**	**Comentarios**	**Puerta**
U.S. Air	750	San Juan	10:55	11:15	2
Avianca	615	Bogotá	11:40	a tiempo	3
VIASA	357	Miami/N.Y.	14:20	a tiempo	7
Aeroméxico	511	México	15:00	14:00	9

1. —Información.

   —¿______________________________?

   —Llega a las 12:45.

   —¿______________________________?

   —No, llega a tiempo.

2. —Información.

   —Quisiera saber si hay retraso con el vuelo de VIASA a Miami.

   —______________________________

   —¿A qué hora sale y de qué puerta?

   —______________________________

   —Por favor, una pregunta más. ¿Cuál es el número del vuelo?

   —______________________________

   —Gracias.

   —______________________________

Actividad 14 **El itinerario.** You work at a travel agency. Refer to the accompanying itinerary to answer the questions from the agency's clients. Use complete sentences.

ITINERARIO DE VUELOS			
DESDE CARACAS	**Nº de Vuelo**	**Hora**	**Día**
Caracas/Maracaibo	620	7:00	miércoles/sábado
Caracas/Porlamar	600	21:00	viernes/domingo
Caracas/Ciudad de Panamá*/ San Juan Pto. Rico	610	16:55	viernes
Caracas/Barcelona	614	21:00	viernes
HACIA CARACAS	**Nº de Vuelo**	**Hora**	**Día**
Maracaibo/Caracas	621	19:00	miércoles/sábado
Porlamar/Caracas	601	22:25	viernes/domingo
Barcelona/Caracas	611	18:20	viernes
Barcelona/Caracas	615	22:25	viernes

*Cambio de avión

1. —Quiero ir de Caracas a Barcelona el sábado. ¿Es posible?

   —______________________________

2. —¿Puedo ir de Maracaibo a Caracas el lunes que viene?

   —______________________________

3. —¿Qué días y a qué horas puedo viajar de Porlamar a Caracas?

   —______________________________

   ____

4. —¿Hay un vuelo directo de Caracas a San Juan?

   —______________________________

   —¿Dónde hace escala?

   —______________________________

   —¿Tengo que cambiar de avión o solo hace escala?

   —______________________________

   —Bueno, entonces voy a comprar un pasaje.

Continued on next page →

Nombre ______________________ Sección ______________ Fecha ____________

—¿Tiene Ud. pasaporte y visa para entrar en los Estados Unidos? ¿Y cuánto tiempo hace que sacó su pasaporte y la visa?

—____

____

Gramática para la comunicación II

Indicating Time and Age in the Past: *Ser* and *tener*

Actividad 15 **¿Qué hora era?** State what time it was when the following actions took place.

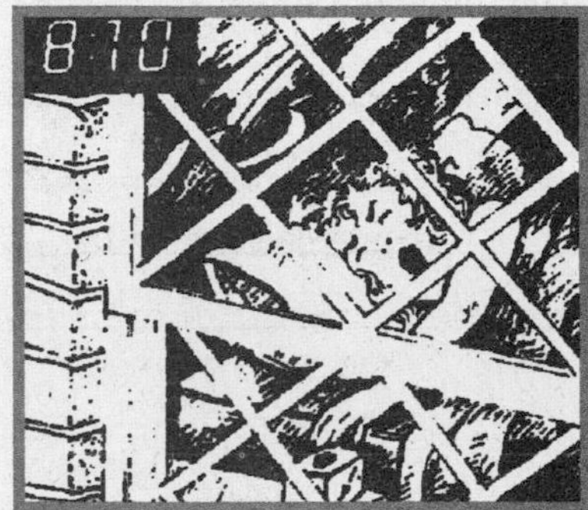

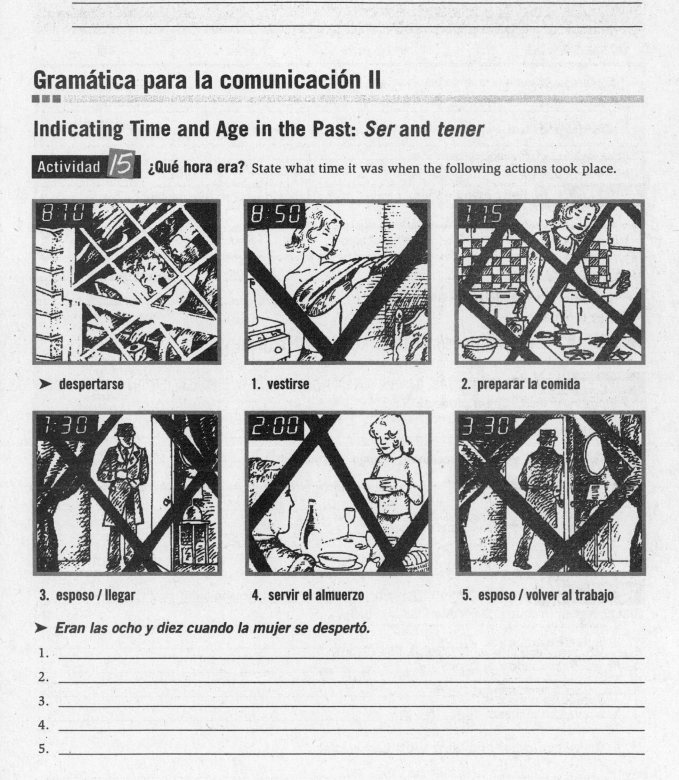

➤ **despertarse**

1. vestirse

2. preparar la comida

3. esposo / llegar

4. servir el almuerzo

5. esposo / volver al trabajo

➤ ***Eran las ocho y diez cuando la mujer se despertó.***

1. ____
2. ____
3. ____
4. ____
5. ____

Actividad 16 **¿Cuántos años tenías?** Answer these questions about you and your family.

1. ¿Cuántos años tenías cuando terminaste la escuela primaria? ______________________________
____
2. ¿Cuántos años tenías cuando recibiste tu primera bicicleta? ______________________________
____
3. ¿Cuántos años tenías cuando empezaste la universidad? ______________________________
____
4. ¿Cuántos años tenías cuando George W. Bush subió a la presidencia por segunda vez en el año 2005?
____

Actividad 17 **Feliz cumpleaños.** Answer the following questions in complete sentences.

1. ¿Cuántos años tenía tu madre cuando tú naciste (*were born*)? ______________________________
____
2. ¿Y tu padre? ______________________________
3. ¿Qué hora era cuando tú naciste? ______________________________

Avoiding Redundancies: Direct-Object Pronouns

Actividad 18 ***Lo, la, los, las.*** Rewrite the following sentences, replacing the direct object with the appropriate direct-object pronoun.

1. No veo a Juan. ______________________________
2. No tenemos los libros. ______________________________
3. Elisa está comprando comida. ______________________________
4. No conoció a tu padre. ______________________________
5. Juan y Nuria no trajeron a sus primos. ______________________________
6. Vamos a comprar papas fritas. ______________________________

Actividad 19 **De otra manera.** Rewrite the following sentences in a different manner without changing their meaning. Make all necessary changes.

1. Tengo que comprarlos. ______________________________
2. Te estoy invitando a la fiesta. ______________________________
3. Lo estamos escribiendo. ______________________________
4. Van a vernos mañana. ______________________________

Nombre ______________________ Sección ______________ Fecha ____________

Actividad 20 **Pronombres de complemento directo.** Answer the following questions in complete sentences, using direct-object pronouns.

1. ¿Me quieres? ______________________
2. ¿Vas a traer los pasajes? ______________________
3. ¿Nos estás invitando? ______________________
4. ¿Llevas la maleta? ______________________
5. ¿Compraste la pasta de dientes? ______________________

Actividad 21 **La respuesta apropiada.** Construct a logical conversation by selecting the correct options.

CLIENTE Quiero ver estas blusas, pero en azul.

VENDEDORA
a. ☐ Aquí los tienes.
b. ☐ No las tenemos en azul.
c. ☐ No la tengo.

CLIENTE
a. ☐ Entonces, en otro color.
b. ☐ Pues, deseo verlo en rosado.
c. ☐ Bueno, si no hay en otro color, quiero azul.

VENDEDORA
a. ☐ Las tengo en color rosado.
b. ☐ Voy a ver si los tengo en amarillo.
c. ☐ Sí, hay mucha.

CLIENTE
a. ☐ Este es muy elegante. Lo llevo.
b. ☐ No me gusta este. Lo siento.
c. ☐ Esta es muy bonita. La voy a llevar.

VENDEDORA
a. ☐ ¿La va a pagar?
b. ☐ ¿Cómo va a pagarla?
c. ☐ ¿Cómo va a pagarlas?

CLIENTE
a. ☐ Las pago con la tarjeta de crédito.
b. ☐ La pago con la tarjeta Visa.
c. ☐ No, no voy a pagarla.

Actividad 22 **Las definiciones.** Write definitions for the following objects without naming the objects themselves. To do this, you will need to use direct-object pronouns, as shown in the example. Remember that the word **it** is never expressed as a subject in Spanish.

➤ libros ***Los compramos para las clases. Los usamos cuando estudiamos.***
Tienen mucha información. Son de papel.
Los leo todas las noches. Me gustan mucho.

1. computadora ____
____
____

2. pantalones ____
____
____

Un poco de todo

Actividad 23 **Una conversación.** Read this conversation between two friends who haven't seen each other in a long time. After reading it, go back and fill in each missing word with a logical verb from the list in the appropriate present, preterit, or imperfect. Do not repeat any verbs.

dar	estar	mentir	tener
decir	explicar	pedir	trabajar
escribir	ir	ser	ver

MARTA Hace ocho años que te ______________ por última vez. ¿Cómo estás?

ANTONIO Bien. ¿Todavía ______________ en el banco?

MARTA No, te ______________ un email hace dos años donde te ______________ todo.

ANTONIO Ah sí, tú les ______________ un cambio (*change*) de oficina a tus jefes.

MARTA Exacto. Entonces me ______________ que sí, pero nunca me ______________ una oficina nueva.

ANTONIO Así que ellos te ______________.

MARTA Sí, y yo ______________ a trabajar en una compañía de electrónica. Increíble ¿no? ______________ 52 años cuando hice todo eso.

ANTONIO ¿______________ contenta ahora?

MARTA Muy contenta. El trabajo ______________ maravilloso.

Lectura

Estrategia de lectura: Identifying Main Ideas

As you read in your textbook, main ideas can be found in titles, headings, or subheadings and also in topic sentences, which many times begin a paragraph or a section of a reading. Other important or supporting ideas can be found in the body of a paragraph or section.

In the following reading about lodging in Spain, each section is introduced by a title and a topic sentence.

Actividad 24 **Alojamiento en tu país.** Before reading, make a list of different types of lodging available in your country for tourists. You can make this list in English.

____

____

Actividad 25 **Un esquema.** Fill in the boxes and the blanks with the titles of the sections, the topic sentences, and the supporting evidence provided.

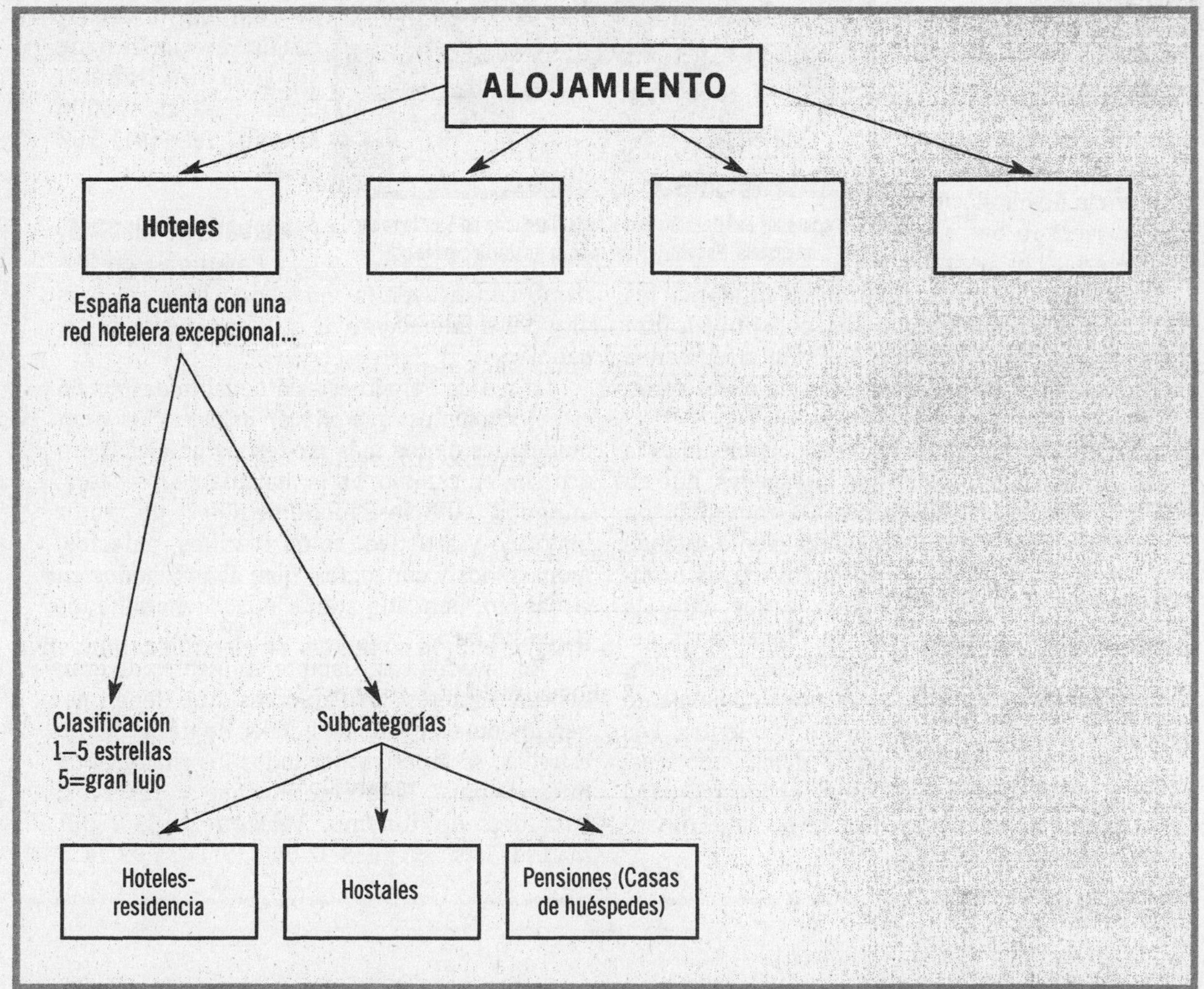

ALOJAMIENTO

HOTELES

España cuenta con una red hotelera excepcional por el número, la variedad y la calidad de unos establecimientos que se reparten por toda la geografía de nuestro país, y que son capaces de adaptarse a cualquier exigencia y posibilidad.

Los hoteles españoles están clasificados en cinco categorías, que se identifican con un número de estrellas que va de una a cinco, según los servicios y las características de cada uno. Existe también un reducido número de hoteles de cinco estrellas, de características auténticamente excepcionales, que ostentan además la categoría máxima de GRAN LUJO.

Los denominados **hoteles-residencia,** que se rigen por la misma clasificación que los demás hoteles, son aquellos que carecen de restaurante, aunque sirven desayunos, tienen servicio de habitaciones y poseen un bar o una cafetería. Los **hostales,** establecimientos de naturaleza similar a los hoteles, pero más modestos, constituyen otra modalidad de alojamiento. Están clasificados en tres categorías que van de una a tres estrellas.

El comedor del Parador Los Reyes Católicos en Santiago de Compostela, España. ¿A un niño le gustaría comer allí?

Otra posible modalidad de alojamiento es la constituida por las **casas de huéspedes,** que en España se llaman **pensiones.** De gran tradición en nuestro país, resultan generalmente establecimientos acogedores y cómodos, cuyas instalaciones y servicios pueden variar entre la sobriedad y un lujo relativo. Regentados generalmente por la familia propietaria de la casa, su precio suele incluir solamente el alojamiento y las comidas, frecuentemente excelentes. Las pensiones resultan un tipo de alojamiento ideal para los visitantes que deseen conocer España en profundidad, apartándose de las rutas turísticas más frecuentadas.

CAMPINGS

España cuenta con cerca de 800 campings, que reúnen una capacidad global de casi 400.000 plazas. Repartidos por todo el terreno nacional, son especialmente abundantes en las costas, y están clasificados en diversas categorías según sus características e instalaciones, como los hoteles. Sus tarifas varían en función de la cantidad y calidad de sus servicios. En el caso de que se opte por hacer acampada libre es recomendable informarse previamente acerca de la no existencia de prohibiciones municipales que afecten al lugar elegido. Si se desea acampar en un terreno privado, es preciso obtener previamente el permiso del propietario.

La Federación Española de Empresarios de Campings y Ciudades de Vacaciones tiene su sede en General Oráa 52-2°D, 28006 Madrid. Tel.: (91) 562 99 94.

PARADORES DE TURISMO

Los Paradores de Turismo constituyen la modalidad hotelera más original e interesante de la oferta turística española.

La red de Paradores está constituida por 86 establecimientos, que ofrecen los servicios y comodidades de los más modernos hoteles, pero ocupan, en cambio, en la mayoría de los casos, antiguos edificios monumentales de valor histórico y artístico, como castillos, palacios, monasterios y conventos, que, abandonados en el pasado, han sido adquiridos y rehabilitados para este fin.

Enclavados casi siempre en lugares de gran belleza e interés, los Paradores, que tienen generalmente categoría de hoteles de tres o cuatro estrellas, se reparten por todos los rincones de nuestro país. Para información y reservas: Paradores de Turismo, Velázquez 18, 28001 Madrid. Tels.: (91) 435 97 00 y (91) 435 97 44.

Nombre ______________________ Sección ______________ Fecha ____________

Actividad 26 **El alojamiento en España.** After reading the article, answer the following questions about lodging in Spain.

1. ¿Cuál es más impersonal, un hotel-residencia o una pensión? ¿Por qué? ______________________

   ____

2. ¿Dónde hay más lugares para hacer camping? ¿En el centro de España o en la costa?

   ____

3. ¿Cuántos Paradores hay? ¿En qué tipo de edificios están? ¿Cómo son generalmente los lugares donde están?

   ____

   ____

4. ¿Dónde te gustaría pasar una noche: en un hostal, una pensión, un camping o en un Parador? ¿Por qué?

   ____

   ____

   ____

Capítulo 7 Repaso

The Details

Look at the following sentences and note how the use of an article (**el/un, la/una**) or lack of one can change the meaning.

Voy a comprar **la chaqueta** que vimos ayer.	The speaker has a specific one in mind.
Voy a comprar **una chaqueta** para el invierno.	The speaker has none in mind; he/she will go to some stores and just look for one.
Mañana voy a comer en **el restaurante** Casa Pepe.	The speaker has a specific one in mind—Casa Pepe.
Mañana voy a comer en **el restaurante**.	Implying the specific one the speaker has in mind.
Mañana voy a comer en **un restaurante** chino.	The speaker will eat in a Chinese restaurant, but does not specify which.
Yo como en **restaurantes** con frecuencia.	Implying that the speaker goes to many different restaurants.

Look at how the use of **el/los** can change the meaning in these sentences.

Trabajo **el** lunes. On Monday
Trabajo **los** lunes. On Mondays

Note the use of these prepositions in Spanish:

Estudio **en** la universidad de Georgetown.
Para mí, la clase **de** literatura moderna es muy difícil.
Normalmente estudio **por** la tarde.
Tengo que terminar un trabajo **para** el viernes.

Remember all the uses of **a**:

- the personal **a**
  Conozco **a** mi profesor de biología muy bien.
- before an indirect object (as with **gustar**)
  A Juan y **a** Verónica les gusta la clase de biología.
  Le doy el trabajo **al** profesor.

Nombre ______________________________ Sección ________________ Fecha ____________

- **a** + *place*

  asistir a + *place/event,* **ir a** + *place/event*
  Asisto a mi clase de español todos los días.
  Voy a la universidad temprano todos los días.

- verbs that take **a** before infinitives

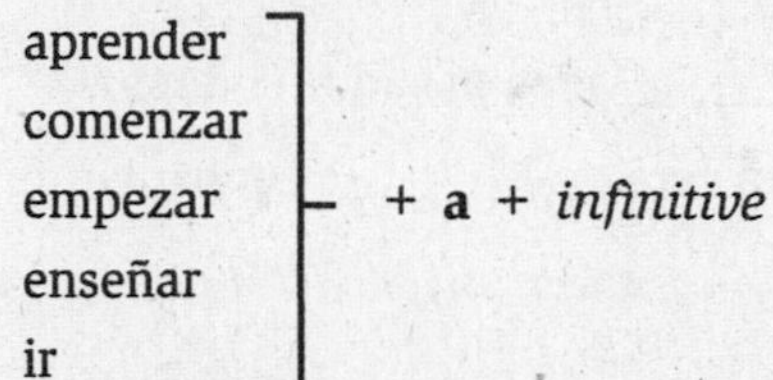

Poco a poco **aprendo a escribir** español.
Empiezo a entender las conversaciones del programa de laboratorio.
El profesor nos **enseña a pronunciar** las palabras correctamente.

Actividad 7 **Conversaciones.** Complete the following conversations with the correct articles or prepositions. Only one word per blank.

1. —Mi padre está __________ __________ hospital.

   —¿Cuándo va __________ salir?

   —__________ miércoles, si Dios quiere.

2. —¡Carlitos! ¿Cuándo vas __________ aprender __________ comer bien?

   —Mamá, mamá, Ramón me está molestando.

3. —No quiero asistir __________ la reunión.

   —Yo tampoco. ¿Por qué no vamos __________ __________ restaurante __________ el centro?

   —Buena idea. Yo conozco __________ restaurante muy bueno.

4. —Por fin empiezo __________ entenderte.

   —¿Aprendiste __________ leer mis pensamientos?

   —No dije eso.

5. —¿Dónde estudias?

   —__________ la Universidad Autónoma.

   —¿Cuándo empezaste?

   —Empecé __________ estudiar allí hace tres años.

   —¿Qué estudias?

   —Arte.

   —¿__________ tus padres les gusta __________ idea?

   —Claro, ¡son artistas!

Continued on next page →

6. — Oye, voy _________ tener el carro _________ Felipe este fin de semana.

— ¿Adónde quieres ir?

— Me gustaría ir _________ _________ capital. ¿Podemos ir?

— ¿Por qué no? Voy _________ ver _________ Pilar mañana _________ la noche.

— ¿Y?

— Y su hermano comenzó _________ trabajar en la capital _________ mes pasado. Podemos dormir _________ el apartamento _________ él. Creo que está cerca _________ centro y que es muy grande.

— Buena idea.

7. — ¿Compraste _________ saco que vimos _________ otro día?

— Sí, me costó _________ ojo de la cara.

— Ahora necesitas corbata.

— Sí, _________ corbata _________ seda roja.

8. — ¿_________ cuándo es la composición?

— Es _________ _________ lunes.

Nombre ______________________ Sección ______________ Fecha ____________

Capítulo 8 La comida y los deportes

Vocabulario esencial I

La comida

Actividad 1 **La palabra que no pertenece.** Select the word that doesn't belong.

1. aceite, ensalada, servilleta, vinagre
2. arvejas, cordero, habichuelas, espárragos
3. pavo, bistec, chuleta, carne de res
4. cuchillo, tenedor, taza, cuchara
5. ternera, ajo, cordero, cerdo
6. tomate, maíz, papa, cuenta
7. lentejas, coliflor, frijoles, arvejas
8. fruta, helado, zanahorias, flan
9. plato, copa, vaso, taza
10. coliflor, espinacas, cebolla, ajo

Actividad 2 **La mesa.** Look at the following drawing and label the items. Remember to include the definite article in your answers.

Actividad 3 **Una cena especial.** You are planning a dinner party at a restaurant for your parents' wedding anniversary. The restaurant manager suggests ordering two dishes for the first course, two dishes for the second, and something for dessert; that way your guests will have choices. You also need to plan a special vegetarian menu for your aunt and uncle. You can spend up to 30 euros per person. Look at the menu and complete the restaurant order form.

Mi Buenos Aires Querido

Casa del Churrasco
Castellana 240, Madrid

Primer plato	*euros*
Sopa de verduras	6,00
Espárragos con mayonesa	7,00
Salmón ahumado	8,20
Tomate relleno	6,00
Ensalada rusa (papas, arvejas, zanahorias)	5,80
Provoleta (queso provolone con orégano)	6,00
Segundo plato	
Churrasco	16,00
Bistec de ternera con puré de papas	15,00
Medio pollo al ajo con papas fritas	13,00
Ravioles de queso	10,00
Lasaña	10,00
Pan	2,00

Ensaladas	*euros*
Mixta	6,00
Zanahoria y huevo	6,00
Waldorf	7,00
Bebidas	
Agua con o sin gas	3,00
Media botella	2,00
Gaseosas	3,00
Té	2,50
Café	2,50
Vino tinto, blanco	4,00
Postres	
Helado de vainilla, chocolate	6,20
Flan con dulce de leche	6,20
Torta de chocolate	7,80
Frutas de estación	5,50
Menú del día	
ensalada mixta, medio pollo al ajo con papas, postre, café y pan	25,00

Primer plato 1. ______
2. ______
Segundo plato 1. ______
2. ______
Postre ______
Champán ☐ Sí ☐ No
Vino, agua, pan y café incluidos en el precio para grupos de veinticinco o más.

Señor Jiménez:

También necesitamos un menú especial para vegetarianos, que va a incluir lo siguiente:

Primer plato ______
Segundo plato ______
Postre ______

Nombre ______________________ Sección ______________ Fecha ____________

Actividad 4 **Rompecabezas.** Do the following newspaper puzzle. By finding the correct word for each definition, you will be able to complete a popular Spanish saying that means *he's blushing.*

1. Es verde y es la base de la ensalada. _ _ _ _ _ _ _ (1, 10)
2. Lloro cuando corto esta verdura; es blanca. _ _ _ _ _ _ _ (8, 6)
3. Lo uso en la cocina y en mi carro. _ _ _ _ _ _ (4)
4. A Popeye le gusta comer esto mucho. _ _ _ _ _ _ _ _ _ (2)
5. Una banana es parte de este grupo. _ _ _ _ _ _ (3)
6. En una ensalada pongo aceite y esto. _ _ _ _ _ _ _ (11)
7. Son rojos, negros o marrones y se ponen en los burritos. _ _ _ _ _ _ _ _ (7)
8. Para comer uso una cuchara, un cuchillo y esto. _ _ _ _ _ _ _ (5)
9. Es la compañera de la sal; es negra. _ _ _ _ _ _ _ _ (9)

El dicho secreto: _ _ _ _   _ _ _ _   _ _ _ _
1 2 3 4   5 6 7 6   8 6 9 6

_ _   _ _ _ _ _ _
10 11   3 6 9 4 3 1

Grámatica para la comunicación I

Expressing Likes, Dislikes, and Opinions: Using Verbs Like *Gustar*

Actividad 5 **Verbos como *gustar*.** Complete the following sentences with the correct form of the indicated verb. (Some function like **gustar** and need an indirect-object pronoun; others do not.)

1. A mí ______________________ que estás loca. (parecer)
2. A Bernardo y a Amalia ______________________ las películas viejas. (fascinar)
3. ¿A ti ______________________ tiempo para terminar la tarea? (faltar)
4. El Sr. Castañeda nunca ______________________ trabajar porque es millonario. (necesitar)
5. Ahora, después de caminar tanto hoy, a Gustavo ______________________ los zapatos. (molestar)
6. Ayer a Julio ______________________ el concierto. (fascinar)
7. ¿Por qué no me ______________________ cuando te pedí ayuda? (ayudar)
8. A Amparo siempre ______________________ dinero. (faltar)

Actividad 6 **La universidad.** You just received a questionnaire about university life. Answer the following questions, using complete sentences.

1. ¿Cuáles son tres cosas que te fascinan de esta universidad? ______
2. ¿Cuáles son tres cosas que te molestan? ______
3. ¿Te parecen excelentes, buenas, regulares o malas las clases? ______
4. ¿Te parece excelente, buena, regular o mala la comida? ______
5. ¿Te parece que hay suficientes computadoras en la universidad para hacer investigación (*research*)? ______
6. ¿Te falta algo en la universidad? ______

Algún comentario personal:

______

Avoiding Redundancies: Combining Direct- and Indirect-Object Pronouns

Actividad 7 **Combina.** Rewrite the following sentences, using direct- and indirect-object pronouns.

1. Te voy a escribir una carta de amor. ______
2. Le regalé dos discos compactos de rock. ______
3. Mi madre les pidió una sopa de verduras. ______
4. ¿Te mandé los papeles? ______
5. Estoy preparándote un café. ______

Actividad 8 **De otra manera.** Rewrite the following sentences that contain direct- and indirect-object pronouns without changing their meaning. Pay attention to accents.

➤ ¿Me lo vas a preparar? ***¿Vas a preparármelo?***

1. Te lo voy a comprar. ______
2. Se la estoy escribiendo. ______
3. Me los tienes que lavar. ______
4. Nos lo está leyendo. ______
5. ¿Se lo puedes mandar? ______

Continued on next page →

6. Te las va a preparar. ______________________________
7. ¿Me lo estás pidiendo? ______________________________
8. Se los vamos a traer. ______________________________

Actividad 9 **El esposo histérico.** Your friend Víctor is preparing a romantic dinner for his wife's return from a long business trip and you are helping him. Víctor is very nervous and wants everything to be perfect. Complete the conversation between you and Víctor, using direct- and indirect-object pronouns when possible.

VÍCTOR Gracias por tu ayuda. ¿Me compraste el vino blanco?

TÚ Sí, ______________________________

VÍCTOR ¿Pusiste las flores en la mesa?

TÚ ______________________________

VÍCTOR ¿Me limpiaste el baño?

TÚ Sí, esta mañana ______________________________

VÍCTOR ¿Qué crees? ¿Debo ponerme corbata?

TÚ ______________________________

VÍCTOR ¡Ay! Tengo los zapatos sucios (*dirty*).

TÚ ¡Tranquilo, hombre! Yo voy a ______________________________ ¿Por qué no te sientas y miras la televisión? Tu esposa no llega hasta las tres. Te voy a preparar un té.

Using *ya* and *todavía*

Actividad 10 **¿Ya o todavía?** Complete the following sentences, using **ya** or **todavía.**

1. Mi madre ______________ sabe qué va a preparar para la cena: arroz con pollo.
2. ______________ no tenemos carro, pero vamos a comprar uno mañana.
3. La gente ______________ votó en las elecciones. ¡Hay un presidente nuevo!
4. ______________ tengo que hablar con mis padres; esta mañana no contestaron el teléfono.
5. ¡¡¡¡SHHHH!!!! El bebé ______________ está dormido, pero se va a despertar pronto.
6. Carolina me dijo lo que pasó. ______________ sé la verdad.
7. Limpié la casa, preparé la comida y la sangría, compré el pastel. ______________ no tengo que hacer nada más para la fiesta.
8. ¡Hombre, claro! ______________ entiendo.
9. ______________ no entiendo. ¿Puedes repetirlo?

Actividad 11 **Las actividades de esta semana.** Look at the following list and state what things you have already done and what things you still have to do this week. Use **ya** or **todavía** in your responses.

➤ invitar a Juan a la fiesta ***Ya lo invité.***
Todavía tengo que invitarlo.

1. estudiar para el examen ______
2. comprar pasta de dientes ______
3. escribirle una carta a mi abuelo ______
4. hablar por teléfono con mis padres ______
5. ir al laboratorio de español ______
6. aprender las formas del imperfecto ______
7. sacar dinero del banco ______
8. comprarle un regalo a mi novio/a ______

Un poco de todo

Actividad 12 **El primer mes. Parte A:** Answer these questions about your first month at college. Use object pronouns when possible.

1. ¿Tus padres te mandaron dinero? ______
2. ¿Te mandó comida tu abuela? ¿Qué te mandó? ______
3. ¿Les escribiste cartas a tus abuelos? ______
4. ¿Les mandaste fotos digitales a tus padres? ______
5. Para su cumpleaños, ¿les mandaste tarjetas (*cards*) virtuales a tus amigos de la escuela secundaria o les compraste tarjetas de Hallmark? ______
6. ¿Le dijiste tus problemas a tu compañero/a de cuarto? ¿Te escuchó? ______
7. ¿Los profesores te dieron ayuda extra? ______
8. ¿La universidad les ofreció a los estudiantes nuevos programas especiales de orientación? ¿Asististe a estos programas? ______
9. ¿Qué cosas te gustaron de tu nueva vida? ______

Continued on next page →

Nombre ______________________ Sección ______________ Fecha ____________

Parte B: Now that you have been at the university for a while, answer these questions.

1. ¿Tus padres todavía te mandan dinero? ______________________

2. ¿Todavía hablas con tus amigos de la escuela secundaria con mucha frecuencia? ______________________

3. ¿Ya eres experto/a o todavía hay más que tienes que aprender sobre cómo funciona la universidad? ______________________

4. ¿Te pareció fácil o difícil adaptarte a la vida universitaria? ______________________

Vocabulario esencial II

Los artículos de deportes

Actividad 13 Los deportes. Match the sports-related items in Column A with the sports in Column B. Write all possible answers.

A	B
1. cascos _______	a. béisbol
2. uniformes _______	b. basquetbol
3. pelotas _______	c. fútbol
4. bates _______	d. fútbol americano
5. raquetas _______	e. tenis
6. guantes _______	f. bolos
7. palos _______	g. golf
8. estadio _______	h. boxeo
9. balón _______	i. ciclismo

Actividad 14 Tus deportes favoritos. State what sports you do and what items you have or don't have to play those sports.

➤ ***Me gusta jugar al basquetbol, pero no tengo balón y por eso siempre usamos el balón de mi amigo Chris.***

____

____

____

Grámatica para la comunicación II

Describing in the Past: The Imperfect

Actividad 15 **¿Qué hacíamos?** Complete the sentences with the appropriate imperfect form of the indicated verbs.

1. Todos los días, yo ____________ a la escuela. (ir)
2. Mi familia siempre ____________ a la una y media. (comer)
3. Todos los martes y jueves después de trabajar, ellos ____________ al fútbol en un equipo. (jugar)
4. Cuando yo ____________ pequeño, mi madre ____________ en un hospital. (ser, trabajar)
5. Cuando mis abuelos ____________ veinte años, no ____________ DVDs. (tener, haber)
6. Pablo Picasso ____________ todos los días. (pintar)
7. John F. Kennedy, Jr. ____________ muy guapo. (ser)
8. De pequeño, mi hermano nos ____________ muchas cosas. (preguntar)
9. Todos los veranos, mi primo y yo ____________ en torneos de tenis. Nosotros no ____________ mucho, pero siempre ____________. (participar, ganar, divertirse)

Actividad 16 **Todos los días.** Complete the sentences with the appropriate imperfect form of the indicated verbs. As you have learned, the imperfect is used for habitual past actions, recurring past events, or to describe in the past. After completing the sentence, write **H/R** if the sentence describes habitual past actions or recurring past events and **D** for past description.

H/R or D

1. Nuestra casa ____________ grande y ____________ cinco dormitorios. (ser, tener) ______
2. Todos los viernes nosotros ____________ al cine. (ir) ______
3. Todos los días, mis amigos y yo ____________ al tenis y yo siempre ____________. (jugar, perder) ______
4. De pequeño, Pablo ____________ mucho y ahora es médico. (estudiar) ______
5. Francisco Franco ____________ bajo, un poco gordo y ____________ bigote. (ser, tener) ______
6. En la escuela secundaria, nosotros ____________ a las doce, y después de la escuela ____________ a comer pizza. (almorzar, ir) ______

Continued on next page →

7. Mi madre siempre nos ______________________ a ver películas de Disney. (llevar) ______

8. Todos los días mi ex esposo me ______________________ poesías horribles. (escribir) ______

9. Mi primera novia ______________________ muy inteligente, pero no le __________________ nada la política y a mí me __________________. (ser, gustar, fascinar) ______

Actividad 17 **Mi vida en Santiago.** Complete this description about Mario's life while he was living in Santiago de Chile. Use the imperfect.

Todos los días yo ______________________ (levantarse) temprano para ir a trabajar. ______________________ (caminar) al trabajo porque ______________________ (vivir) muy cerca. ______________________ (Trabajar) en una escuela de inglés y ______________________ (enseñar) cuatro clases al día, un total de veinticuatro horas por semana. Mis estudiantes ______________________ (ser) profesionales que ______________________ (necesitar) el inglés para su trabajo. Todos ______________________ (ser) muy inteligentes e ______________________ (ir) a clase muy bien preparados. Me ______________________ (gustar) mis estudiantes y muchas veces ellos y yo ______________________ (salir) después de las clases. ______________________ (comer) en restaurantes o ______________________ (ir) al cine. Santiago es fantástico y quiero volver algún día.

Un poco de todo

Actividad 18 **Wimbledon. Parte A.** Choose the appropriate verbs from the list to complete the following summary of a tennis match. Write the imperfect form of the verb if there is an **i** and the preterit form if there is a **p**. Note: This and the following activity preview use of the preterit and imperfect together. You will learn more about this in **Capítulo 9.**

decir	esperar	estar	haber	poder	tener
empezar	esperar	ganar	hacer	ser	

Ayer ______________________ (i) mucha gente en el estadio de Wimbledon. ______________________ (i) mucho calor y sol. Entre el público ______________________ (i) Guillermo Vilas, el príncipe Carlos, Marcelo Ríos, Arantxa Sánchez Vicario y otra gente famosa. Todo el mundo ______________________ (i) ver el partido entre el español Rafael Nadal y el argentino Mariano Puerta.

______________________ (i) las dos y media cuando ______________________ (p) el partido; todo el mundo ______________________ (i) en silencio; nadie ______________________ (i) nada, esperando ansiosamente la primera pelota. Después de hora y media de juego en el calor intenso, Nadal ______________________ (p) un accidente y no ______________________ (p) continuar. Así que Mariano Puerta ______________________ (p) el partido.

Continued on next page →

Parte B. Read the paragraph again and answer these questions.

1. Is the imperfect or the preterit used to give past description? ______________________________

2. Is the imperfect or the preterit used to narrate what occurred? ______________________________

Actividad 19 **El robo.** Yesterday you witnessed a theft and you had to go to the police station to make a statement. Look at the drawings and complete the conversation with the police in complete sentences. Use the preterit and the imperfect as cued by the questions.

POLICÍA ¿Qué hora era cuando vio Ud. el robo?

TÚ ____

POLICÍA ¿Dónde estaba Ud. y dónde estaba la víctima?

TÚ ____

POLICÍA ¿Qué hizo específicamente el ladrón *(thief)*?

TÚ ____

____

POLICÍA ¿Cómo era físicamente el ladrón?

TÚ ____

____

POLICÍA ¿Bigote o barba? La víctima nos dijo que tenía barba.

TÚ ____

POLICÍA ¿Y la descripción del carro?

TÚ ____

____

POLICÍA ¿Quién manejaba? ¿Lo vio Ud. bien? ¿Sabe cómo era?

TÚ ____

POLICÍA Muchas gracias por ayudarnos.

Nombre ______________________ Sección ______________ Fecha ____________

Actividad 20 **Los niños de ayer y de hoy.** Diana and Marisel are comparing what they did when they were 13 years old with what 13-year-olds in the U.S. do now. Complete their conversation using the imperfect or the present.

DIANA Cuando yo tenía trece años, ____

____.

MARISEL Yo iba al cine, salía con grupos de amigos y viajaba con mis padres.

DIANA También ____

____.

MARISEL Pero hoy... ¡los adolescentes parecen adultos!

DIANA Sí, es verdad, hoy los jóvenes de la escuela donde enseño en los Estados Unidos ________

____.

MARISEL ¡Es una lástima!

DIANA Pero eso no es todo; también ____

____.

MARISEL Son como pequeños adultos; casi no tienen infancia (*childhood*).

Actividad 21 **¡Cómo cambiamos!** Paulina went to the same high school as you. You saw her yesterday and couldn't believe your eyes; she seems like a different person. Look at the drawings of Paulina and write an email to your friend Hernando. Tell him what Paulina was like and what she used to do (imperfect), and what she is like and what she does now (present).

Antes | Ahora

Asunto: Paulina

Querido Hernando:

No lo vas a creer; acabo de ver a Paulina Mateos. ¿La recuerdas? Recuerdas que

era ____

____

____

____

____

Pues ahora ____

____

____

____

Un abrazo,

____

Lectura

Estrategia de lectura: Finding References

Understanding the relationship between words and sentences can help improve your understanding of a text. A text is usually full of pronouns and other words that are used to avoid redundancies. Common examples are possessive adjectives; demonstrative adjectives and pronouns; and subject, indirect-, and direct-object pronouns. Furthermore, as you have seen, subject pronouns are generally omitted where the context allows it.

You will have a chance to practice identifying referents (the word or phrase to which a pronoun refers) while you read the next selection.

Actividad 22 **¿Qué sabes?** Before reading, answer the following questions without consulting anyone.

1. Mira el mapa en la contratapa (*inside cover*) de tu libro de texto y escribe qué países forman Centroamérica. ______________________________
____
2. ¿Sabes qué país construyó el Canal de Panamá? ¿Sabes qué país lo administra? ______________________________
____
3. ¿Qué aprendiste sobre Costa Rica en este capítulo? ______________________________
____
4. ¿Qué sabes sobre la situación política de Centroamérica? ______________________________
____

Actividad 23 **Referencias.** While you read the passage, write what the following words or phrases refer to.

1. línea 4: **esa región** ______________________________
2. línea 10: **lo** ______________________________
3. línea 16: **su** ______________________________
4. línea 21: **sus** ______________________________
5. línea 26: **Allí** ______________________________
6. línea 28: **ellos** ______________________________
7. línea 31: **Estas** ______________________________

Nombre ______________________ Sección ______________ Fecha ____________

CENTROAMÉRICA: MOSAICO GEOGRÁFICO Y CULTURAL

Los siete países que forman Centroamérica unen dos gigantes, Norteamérica y Suramérica, y separan el océano Atlántico del océano Pacífico. Seis de ellos son países hispanos; el otro, Belice, es una antigua colonia británica.

Centroamérica es un mosaico de tierras y de pueblos.[1] En **esa región** se encuentran playas blancas, selvas tropicales,[2] montañas de clima fresco, sabanas[3] fértiles y volcanes gigantescos. Su población incluye indígenas con lenguas y algunas costumbres precolombinas, descendientes de europeos, negros, mestizos, mulatos y también asiáticos.

El país más austral[4] de Centroamérica es Panamá, que tiene la mayor población negra de los países hispanos de la región. El recurso económico más importante de ese país es el Canal de Panamá que construyeron los Estados Unidos. El gobierno estadounidense **lo** administró hasta el año 2000, cuando pasó a manos de Panamá. Este canal es de gran importancia comercial porque, al conectar el océano Pacífico con el océano Atlántico, es la ruta ideal para los barcos que van no solo de Nueva York a California sino también de Europa a Asia.

En Costa Rica, la mayoría de la población es de origen europeo y el porcentaje de analfabetismo es bajo (4%). Es un país que no tiene ejército[5] y, además, no tiene grandes conflictos políticos internos. En 1987, el presidente Óscar Arias recibió el Premio Nobel de la Paz por **su** iniciativa en buscar un fin a las guerras[6] de Centroamérica.

Nicaragua, Honduras y El Salvador, por otro lado, son países de grandes conflictos políticos internos, pero a la vez de grandes riquezas naturales. Nicaragua es un país de volcanes donde solo se cultiva el 10% de la tierra. Honduras es un país montañoso; su población vive principalmente en zonas rurales y **sus** exportaciones principales son el banano, el café y la madera. El Salvador, a pesar de ser el país más pequeño de la región, es el tercer exportador de café del mundo, después de Brasil y Colombia. El Salvador es además un país muy densamente poblado. La población de Nicaragua, Honduras y El Salvador tiene un alto porcentaje de mestizos (70%–90%).

Al norte de El Salvador está Guatemala. **Allí** se encuentran ruinas de una de las civilizaciones precolombinas más avanzadas, la civilización maya. Más de un 50% de los guatemaltecos son descendientes directos de los mayas y hablan una variedad de lenguas indígenas; **ellos** forman la población indígena de sangre pura más grande de Centroamérica.

A pesar de las grandes diferencias que existen entre los países centroamericanos, también hay muchas semejanzas. **Estas** forman la base de lo que es Centroamérica, pero, realmente, es la diversidad la que le da riqueza a esta región.

[1]*peoples* [2]*tropical rainforests* [3]*plains* [4]*southernmost* [5]*army* [6]*wars*

Actividad 24 **Preguntas.** Now, answer the following questions, using complete sentences.

1. ¿Cuál es la importancia del Canal de Panamá?

____

2. ¿En qué se diferencia Costa Rica de los otros países centroamericanos?

____

____

3. ¿Qué peculiaridad caracteriza a Nicaragua, Honduras y El Salvador?

____

____

4. ¿Cuál es una característica particular de Guatemala? ______________________

____

Nombre ______________________ Sección ______________ Fecha ______________

Capítulo 9 Cosas que ocurrieron

Vocabulario esencial I

La salud

Actividad 1 **¿Buena salud?** Unscramble the following letters to form health-related words. Write accents where necessary.

1. nacaamubil ______________
2. gernsa ______________
3. igper ______________
4. nfniieócc ______________
5. clseoísraof ______________
6. irrdaea ______________
7. ssáneau ______________
8. dígraofaari ______________
9. efbire ______________
10. tceorsar ______________
11. gaelair ______________
12. aehidr ______________

La salud, los medicamentos y otras palabras relacionadas

Actividad 2 **Asociaciones.** Match the items from Column A with the medicine-related words in Column B.

A	B
1. ______ X	a. receta médica
2. ______ Contac	b. fractura
3. ______ ACE	c. radiografías
4. ______ Robitussin	d. diarrea
5. ______ 103°F, 39°C	e. dolor de cabeza
6. ______ Pepto-Bismol	f. gotas
7. ______ aspirina	g. jarabe
8. ______ Band-Aid	h. fiebre
9. ______ 2 pastillas por día por 1 semana	i. curita
10. ______ Visine	j. cápsulas
	k. vendaje

Actividad 3 **Los remedios.** Complete the following conversation that takes place in a pharmacy.

CLIENTE Tengo un dolor de cabeza terrible.

FARMACÉUTICA ¿Por qué no ______________________________?

CLIENTE ¿Tiene Bayer?

FARMACÉUTICA Claro que sí. ¿Algo más?

CLIENTE Sí, mi hijo tiene un catarro muy fuerte y fiebre.

FARMACÉUTICA Entonces, él tiene que ______________________________.

CLIENTE ¡Ay! No le gustan las cápsulas. ¿No tiene pastillas de Tylenol?

FARMACÉUTICA ______________________________.

CLIENTE También tiene tos.

FARMACÉUTICA Bien, pues debe comprarle ______________________________

______________________________.

CLIENTE Y mi marido se cortó la mano.

FARMACÉUTICA Entonces, ______________________________. ¿Algo más?

CLIENTE Creo que es todo.

FARMACÉUTICA Ya entiendo por qué le duele la cabeza.

Gramática para la comunicación I

Narrating and Describing in the Past: The Preterit and the Imperfect

Actividad 4 **Me jugué la vida. Parte A.** Read the following description of how to use the preterit and imperfect when narrating in the past.

When narrating in the past, if you simply want to list a series of occurrences in the past, you need only the preterit.

Three bears **left** their house.
They **went** to the woods.
A child **arrived** at the house, **knocked** on the door, and **opened** it.
She **entered** the house.

If you want to go beyond the **who did what** (preterit) part of the story, you need to use the imperfect (shown in italics).

There *were* three bears that *lived* in a cute little house in the woods. It *was* a beautiful day. The birds *were singing* and the sun *was shining*. So the three bears **decided** to go for a walk and **left** their house. While they *were enjoying* their walk, a child **appeared** at the house. She *was* young, blond, tired, and hungry. She **knocked** on the door, but no one **answered** because no one *was* home. The door *was* open, so she **went** inside.

In **Part B** you will read a story in English and decide if the verbs should be in the preterit or the imperfect if the story were to be told in Spanish. First, read the following questions and answers; then refer back to them as needed.

Continued on next page →

Nombre ______________________ Sección ______________ Fecha ______________

1. Is this a completed action (similar to a photograph or a finger snap)? If yes, **preterit.**

   The child **knocked** on the door (click/snap)
   She **opened** the door. (click/snap)

2. Does the verb indicate the start or end of an action? If yes, **preterit.**

   The bears **started** their walk at 10:00 and **ended** it at 4:00.

3. Does the verb refer to a completed action that was limited by time? If yes, **preterit.**

   They **walked** for six hours.

4. Does the verb refer to a habitual action or recurring events? If yes, *imperfect.*

   Every day Mama Bear *used to take* Baby Bear for a walk. Every Saturday Papa Bear *went* with them.

5. Does the verb refer to an action or state in progress that is not limited by time? If yes, *imperfect.*

   The bears *lived* in the woods and *were* very happy.

6. Does the verb refer to an action in progress that occurred while another action was happening? If yes, *imperfect.*

   While the bears *walked* (*were walking*) in the woods, the girl *explored* (*was exploring*) their house.

7. Does the verb refer to an action in progress that occurred when another action happened or interrupted it? If yes, *imperfect,* **preterit.**

   While the bears *walked* (*were walking*) in the woods, the girl **broke** a chair.

8. Are you describing in the past? If yes, *imperfect.*

   Baby Bear *was* little, but he *had* big paws and an engaging personality.

9. Time and age in the past are always expressed with the *imperfect.*

   It *was* 4:05 in the afternoon.
   Baby Bear *was* only one year old.

Parte B. The following is a true story about a car accident. As you read it, write **P** for preterit and **I** for imperfect for the indicated verbs.

I was (1) ____ a student in Spain and it was (2) ____ a Friday. I wanted (3) ____ to go to Valencia to visit friends and didn't have (4) ____ a lot of money, so a friend and I decided (5) ____ to hitchhike. Classes ended (6) ____ and I went (7) ____ with my friend to an entrance to the highway to Valencia. It was (8) ____ a beautiful day. We stuck out (9) ____ our thumbs and immediately a car stopped (10) ____ to give us a ride. The car was (11) ____ new and only had (12) ____ 5000 kilometers on the odometer. It was (13) ____ a four-door sedan. My friend sat (14) ____ in the front seat and I sat (15) ____ in the back. The driver was (16) ____ a very nice businessman.

I took off (17) ____ my shoes and soon fell asleep (18) ____ in the back seat. Some time later, we passed (19) ____ a car. We were going (20) ____ quite fast—about 130 kilometers per hour (80 mph), when our car hit (21) ____ a bump in the road and the axle broke (22) ____. The car began (23) ____ to zigzag. We collided (24) ____ head-on with another car. Both cars flew (25) ____ up in the air and

Continued on next page →

our car started (26) _____ to burn. The driver and my friend were (27) _____ unconscious and still in the car. With the impact, my head pushed (28) _____ open the back door and I flew (29) _____ out of the car.

Two couples, who were (30) _____ about 70 years old, were returning (31) _____ from a vacation on the coast when they saw (32) _____ the accident. The men jumped (33) _____ out of their car and ran (34) _____ toward ours. First, they got out (35) _____ the driver. Then they went (36) _____ to get my friend. Her seat was tilted (37) _____ forward and was (38) _____ jammed. Her seatbelt was (39) _____ stuck. One of the men cut (40) _____ the seatbelt with a pocket knife and they finally got (41) _____ her out. While they were pulling (42) _____ her out of the car, one of the men's pants caught fire (43) _____. Then they saw (44) _____ me. I was (45) _____ unconscious on the pavement about 10 meters from the car, but they did not come (46) _____ closer since the car was burning (47) _____. The car never did explode (48) _____. When the fire died down (49) _____, the men came (50) _____ to check on me. I awoke (51) _____ 16 hours later, in a hospital.

Thank goodness no one died (52) _____ in the accident. I spent (53) _____ 17 days in the hospital and then went back (54) _____ to Madrid and returned (55) _____ to my studies.

Today everyone is fine. I only have two little scars as reminders of the accident!

Actividad 5 **¿Imperfecto o pretérito?** Complete the following sentences with the correct preterit or imperfect form of the indicated verbs.

1. Ayer yo ______________________ a un gimnasio nuevo por primera vez. Allí la gente ______________________ gimnasia aeróbica, ______________________ y ______________________ pesas. (ir, hacer, nadar, levantar)
2. De pequeña todos los veranos yo ______________________ un mes en la playa con mi familia. A mí me ______________________. (pasar, encantar)
3. El año pasado durante cuatro meses Manuel y Carmen ______________________ con turistas en Cancún. Por eso, ellos ______________________ un apartamento. (trabajar, alquilar)
4. Todo el sábado pasado ______________________ náuseas y fiebre y por eso no fui a trabajar. (tener)
5. Javier ______________________ a 150 kilómetros por hora cuando lo ______________________ la policía. (manejar, ver)
6. Cuando Roberto me ______________________, yo ______________________ y por eso no ______________________ el teléfono. (llamar, ducharse, contestar)
7. El año pasado cuando nosotros ______________________ por Argentina, ______________________ a un concierto de Les Luthiers. (viajar, ir)

Nombre ______________________ Sección ______________ Fecha ____________

Actividad 6 **¿Qué le pasaba?** Complete this excerpt of an email that don Alejandro and his wife received from their friend in Chile. For each blank, select the appropriate verb from the left margin and write the correct form in the imperfect or preterit.

entrar
estar
tener
levantarse
preparar
pasar
saber
estar

Es increíble el cambio que veo en Nando después de que se casó. Tú sabes que él nunca (1) ______________ en la cocina cuando estaba soltero. Y el viernes pasado yo (2) ______________ por la casa de él para dejarle algo y mientras su esposa Olga miraba la televisión, él (3) ______________ la cena. Cuando él (4) ______________ preparando la ensalada, yo (5) ______________ segura que la ensalada (6) ______________ demasiado vinagre; entonces (7) ______________ del sofá para ayudarlo, pero resulta que Nando (8) ______________ exactamente cómo hacer una ensalada y al final, ¡qué ensalada más deliciosa!

creer
decir
poner
saber
ser
empezar

Olga me (9) ______________ que el otro día mientras ella (10) ______________ la ropa en la lavadora, Nando (11) ______________ a ayudarla. Yo (12) ______________ que él (13) ______________ muy machista (sé que todavía es en ciertos sentidos), pero últimamente está cambiando. Cada día se parece más a su padre. Él tampoco (14) ______________ cocinar antes de casarse.

Actividad 7 **El informe del detective.** You are a private detective and you spent the morning tracking the husband of your client. Using complete sentences, write the report that you are going to give to your client. Say what her husband did during the morning.

trabajar

salir

mientras tomar café / llegar

entrar

mientras probarse vestido / comprar perfume

volver

____

____

____

____

____

____

Actividad 8 **La verdad.** Complete the following conversation between the husband from the previous activity and his wife.

ELLA ¿Qué hiciste hoy?

ÉL Nada; ______________________________.

ELLA ¿Toda la mañana ______________________________?

ÉL Sí, excepto cuando ______________________________ para comprarte esto.

ELLA Un regalo... A ver... ¡Un vestido y un perfume!

ÉL Claro, hoy hace diez años que te ______________________________.

ELLA Es que... es que...

ÉL ¿Quieres decirme algo?

ELLA Es que yo creía que tú ______________________________

______________________________.

ÉL No, ella era ______________________________.

Pero, ¿cómo supiste que fui con ella a la tienda?

Actividad 9 **¿Qué estaban haciendo?** The people in the drawing below heard an explosion and looked toward the street to see what happened. Write what they were doing when they heard the explosion.

➤ El mecánico ***El mecánico estaba trabajando cuando oyó la explosión.***

1. La señora en la ventana ______________________________.
2. Los dos señores en el banco ______________________________.
3. El niño ______________________________.
4. El señor en el balcón ______________________________.
5. La joven en el balcón ______________________________.

Nombre ______________________ Sección ______________ Fecha ____________

Narrating and Describing in the Past: Time Expressions

Actividad 10 **Las vacaciones.** Complete the following sentences about vacations using the preterit or the imperfect. Pay attention to time expressions.

1. De joven, durante los veranos, a menudo ______________ en bicicleta con un grupo de amigos en el parque cerca de mi casa. (montar)
2. Estuve en Puerto Rico una semana en febrero. Todos los días ______________ en la piscina del hotel por la mañana y por la tarde ______________ al golf. (nadar, jugar)
3. Cuando Carlos ______________ en Chile, de vez en cuando ______________ a la playa de Viña del Mar con su familia. (vivir, ir)
4. Todos los años, mi familia ______________ a la casa de mi abuela para la Navidad. Mi abuela ______________ unas comidas espectaculares. (ir, preparar)
5. Después de terminar las negociaciones con Aeroméxico para mi compañía, ______________ cinco días en Oaxaca. Cada día ______________ ruinas diferentes de la zona. (pasar, visitar)

Actividad 11 **El encuentro.** Many people have a strict daily routine and when they do something different, interesting things can happen. Complete this paragraph to tell how Mr. and Mrs. Durán met. Fill in each blank with a logical word or words. Pay attention to the time expressions to help you decide whether to use the preterit or imperfect.

Con frecuencia el Sr. Durán ______________ y muchas veces ______________. Estas actividades eran parte de su rutina diaria. También ______________, ______________ y ______________. Pero el 3 de marzo fue diferente; no ______________. Fue a la playa y allí vio a la Srta. Guzmán. Pensaba que era una mujer muy ______________ y quería conocerla. Mientras ella ______________, él ______________. De repente, ______________ ______________. Así se conocieron y llevan diez años de casados.

Nombre ______________________ Sección ______________ Fecha __________

Un poco de todo

Actividad 12 **Los síntomas.** Complete the following conversations between patients and their doctors.

1. PACIENTE A Hace tres días ______________________________
____
______________________________.

   MÉDICO Creo que Ud. le tiene alergia a algo, pero vamos a hacer unos análisis.

2. PACIENTE B Mi hijo tosía, ______________________________
______________________________.
Ahora está bien, pero no quiere comer.

   DOCTORA Creo que solo fue gripe, pero debe obligarlo a comer algo.

3. PACIENTE C Todas las mañanas ______________________________
______________________________.
Ahora estoy mejor, pero no sé qué me pasaba.

   MÉDICO Vamos a ver. Creo que puede estar embarazada.

Actividad 13 **Un cuento. Parte A.** In this workbook, normally you read a passage and then you answer questions to see if you understood the story. Now you're going to do the opposite. First, read through all the questions that follow. Then use your imagination to answer them.

1. ¿Adónde fueron Ricardo y su esposa de vacaciones? ______________________________
____
2. ¿Cómo era el lugar y qué tiempo hacía? ______________________________
____
3. ¿Qué hicieron durante las vacaciones? ______________________________
____
4. ¿Cómo se murió la esposa de Ricardo? ______________________________
____
5. ¿Qué estaba haciendo Ricardo cuando se rompió la pierna? ______________________________
____
6. La policía no dejó a Ricardo volver a su ciudad. ¿Por qué? ______________________________
____
7. ¿Quién era la señora del vestido negro y los diamantes? ______________________________
____
8. ¿Cómo era físicamente la señora? ______________________________
____

Continued on next page →

Nombre ______________________ Sección ______________ Fecha ____________

9. ¿Qué importancia tiene ella? ____

____

10. Al fin, la policía supo la verdad. ¿Cuál era? ____

____

Parte B. Now create a story based on your answers from Part A. Use the following words and phrases to enhance the telling of your story.

primero	de repente	después
luego/más tarde	mientras	al final
media hora más tarde	después de una hora	

____

____

____

____

____

____

____

____

____

____

____

____

Vocabulario esencial II

El carro

Actividad 14 **El carro.** Identify each numbered automobile part. Include the definite article in your answers.

1. ______________________
2. ______________________
3. ______________________
4. ______________________
5. ______________________
6. ______________________
7. ______________________

Actividad 15 **Problemas, problemas y más problemas.** Complete this letter that Lorenzo Martín wrote to a car rental agency following a terrible experience with a rental car.

Caracas, 15 de febrero de 2006

Estimados señores:

Hace tres semanas, alquilé un carro con transmisión automática en su compañía y tuve muchísimos problemas. Primero, estaba bajando la montaña y de repente noté que no funcionaban muy bien los ______________________. Por suerte no tuve un accidente. Paré en una gasolinera y me los arreglaron. Más tarde empezó a llover, pero no podía ver nada porque el ______________________ del lado del conductor no funcionaba. Después, cuando llegué al hotel, no podía sacar las maletas del ______________________ porque la llave que Uds. me dieron no era la llave que necesitaba; pero por fin un policía me lo abrió. Esa noche salí y no pude ver bien porque una de las ______________________ no funcionaba. Al día siguiente hacía muchísimo calor y el ______________________ no echaba aire frío, solo aire caliente. Y para colmo, me pusieron una ______________________ por exceso de velocidad por ir a 140 kilómetros por hora pero el velocímetro del carro marcaba solo 110.

Hace muchos años que alquilo automóviles de su compañía sin ningún problema; pero después de esta experiencia, creo que voy a tener que ir a otra agencia de alquiler de carros.

Atentamente,

Lorenzo Martín

Gramática para la comunicación II

Narrating and Describing in the Past: *Iba a* and *tenía/tuve que; saber* and *conocer*

Actividad 16 **Las excusas.** Read the following miniconversations. Then complete them, using the preterit or imperfect of **ir** and **tener.** Remember that if you use **tuve/tuvo**/etc. **que** + *infinitive* or **fui**, **fuimos**, etc., it indicates that the action actually took place. The imperfect of **ir a** + *infinitive* means that the action did not take place, and the imperfect of **tener que** + *infinitive* is ambiguous.

1. —Había muchas personas en la fiesta.

   —Entonces, ¿te divertiste?

   —Sí y no. Y tú, ¿dónde estabas? Prometiste venir.

   —______________________ a ir, pero ______________________ que ayudar a mi madre, que estaba enferma.

Continued on next page →

Nombre ______________________ Sección ______________ Fecha __________

2. — ______________ que ir al dentista ayer.

   — ¿Fuiste o no?

   — No fui porque el dentista estaba enfermo.

3. — Nosotros ______________ que ir al banco ayer.

   — ¿Al final ______________ o no?

   — Sí, y el director del banco nos ayudó con un problema que teníamos.

4. — ¿Me compraste el champú?

   — ______________ a comprártelo, pero no ______________ a la tienda porque ______________ un pequeño accidente con el carro.

   — ¡No me digas! ¿Estás bien?

   — ______________ que ir al hospital.

   — ¡Por Dios! ¿Y qué te dijo el médico?

   — No mucho. Estoy bien, solo tengo que tomar aspirinas.

5. — Nosotros ______________ a ir al cine, pero llegamos tarde.

   — Entonces, ¿qué hicieron?

   — Volvimos a casa.

Actividad 17 **¿Pretérito o imperfecto?** Write the correct preterit or imperfect form of the indicated verbs. Remember that the preterit indicates the start of an action; therefore, use the preterit of **saber** to say *I/he/she/etc. found out something* and use the preterit of **conocer** to say *I/you/they/etc. met someone.*

1. El otro día mi novio ______________ a mi padre. (conocer)
2. Ayer yo ______________ la verdad, pero no le ______________ nada a nadie. (saber, decir)
3. Ella no ______________ su número de teléfono, por eso no lo ______________. (saber, llamar)
4. Yo ______________ en Salamanca por tres años, por eso cuando ______________ a esa ciudad el año pasado, no ______________ mapa porque ya ______________ la ciudad muy bien. (vivir, volver, usar, conocer)
5. Margarita ______________ las vacaciones en Hollywood, pero tuvo mala suerte y no ______________ a nadie famoso. (pasar, conocer)
6. Raúl ______________ al profesor Guzmán en enero del año pasado. ______________ con él varias veces sobre sus investigaciones. Así que cuando ______________ a tomar su clase, ya lo ______________ muy bien. (conocer, Hablar, empezar, conocer)

Actividad 18 **La semana pasada.** Write two sentences describing what you were going to do last week, but didn't. Then write two sentences describing what you had to do, but didn't. Finally, tell what you had to do last week and did. Use **iba a** + *infinitive* and **tenía/tuve que** + *infinitive.*

1. ______________________________
2. ______________________________
3. ______________________________
4. ______________________________
5. ______________________________

Describing: Past Participle as an Adjective

Actividad 19 **Descripciones.** Complete the following sentences with the correct past participle form of the indicated verbs.

1. Llegamos tarde y el banco estaba ____________. (cerrar)
2. El niño que perdió su perro está ____________ allí. (sentar)
3. La ropa sucia está en la lavadora y la ropa ____________ está en tu dormitorio. (lavar)
4. Las tiendas están ____________ los domingos, excepto en el centro comercial, donde están ____________ de las doce a las cinco. (cerrar, abrir)
5. María, ¿por qué estás ____________? (preocupar)
6. El contrato estaba ____________, pero nadie quería firmarlo. (escribir)
7. Mi tío vende carros ____________. (usar)
8. Después del accidente, el limpiaparabrisas estaba ____________ y llevamos el carro a un garaje. Ahora el carro está ____________ y ____________. (romper, arreglar, lavar)
9. Los niños están ____________ y ____________. (bañar, vestir)
10. Los niños tienen las manos ____________, la comida está ____________ y la mesa está ____________; ya podemos comer. (lavar, hacer, poner)
11. *Don Quijote de la Mancha* está ____________ a casi todos los idiomas. (traducir)

Nombre ______________________ Sección ______________ Fecha ____________

Actividad 20 **El correo electrónico.** Finish this email message that Alicia sent to Paco, a professional pianist. Use the correct past participle form of the following verbs: **alquilar, morir, preparar, reservar,** and **vender.**

Asunto: Tu viaje

```
Ya está todo listo para tu viaje: La habitación está ________________
en el Hotel Santa Cruz. El carro está ________________ en Hertz.
Todas las entradas están ________________. Todo está
________________ para tu concierto del jueves. ¡Mucha suerte! Después
de tanto trabajo, yo estoy ________________ y creo que voy a dormir
por tres días.
Alicia
```

Un poco de todo

Actividad 21 **Casi se mueren.** Complete these stories about people in risky situations. Write the correct preterit or imperfect form of the indicated verbs.

1. Un amigo, que ________________ celebrando el final de semestre, ________________ mucho en una fiesta. ________________ un poco mareado, pero ________________ la llave del carro de un amigo y ________________ de la fiesta. Por suerte, una persona lo ________________ y otros ________________ para quitarle la llave. Al final, ellos lo ________________ que llevar a casa.

   (estar, beber, Sentirse, tomar, salir, ver, salir, tener)

2. Una amiga ________________ manejando un carro alquilado e ________________ a mucha velocidad cuando un niño ________________ detrás de un balón de fútbol enfrente de su carro. Ella ________________, pero en ese momento los frenos no ________________. Mi amiga no ________________ que el carro ________________ mal los frenos. Por suerte no ________________ al niño, pero ________________ contra un árbol. Gracias a Dios, no le ________________ nada a nadie.

   (estar, ir, correr, frenar, funcionar, saber, tener, atropellar, chocar, pasar)

Actividad 22 **Un email.** Diana wrote the following email to a friend who is a Spanish-language professor in the U.S. Complete her message by choosing a logical verb and writing the infinitive, present participle, or correct form in the present, preterit, or imperfect.

Asunto: Mi vida en Madrid

Querida Vicky:

Ya hace cinco meses que ________________ a España y por fin hoy ________________ unos minutos para ________________ tu email. Las cosas aquí me van de maravilla. Por cuatro meses ________________ en un colegio mayor, pero ahora ________________ un apartamento con cuatro amigas hispanoamericanas. ________________ muy simpáticas y estoy ________________ mucho sobre España y también sobre Hispanoamérica.

(**alquilar, aprender, contestar, llegar, ser, tener, vivir**)

Durante el verano pasado, ________________ clases de arte y arquitectura de lunes a viernes por tres semanas. Por las mañanas, nosotros ________________ a la universidad y por las tardes ________________ museos y lugares históricos como la Plaza Mayor, el Palacio Real y el Convento de las Descalzas Reales. Cuando ________________ por primera vez en el Museo del Prado, me ________________ grandísimo, y solamente ________________ las salas de El Greco y de Velázquez.

(**entrar, ir, parecer, tener, ver, visitar**)

________________ enamorada de España. La música me ________________ porque tiene mucha influencia árabe y gitana (*gypsy*). El otro día ________________ por la calle cuando ________________ a unos niños gitanos cantando y bailando; ________________ unos diez años y ellos me ________________ que, con frecuencia, ________________ en la calle para ________________ dinero.

(**caminar, cantar, decir, estar, fascinar, ganar, tener, ver**)

Mis clases ________________ hace dos meses; después ________________ seis semanas de vacaciones y las clases ________________ otra vez la semana pasada. Además de tomar clases, ________________ enseñando inglés desde junio para ________________ técnicas nuevas de enseñanza. Y tú, ¿cómo estás? ¿Todo bien?

(**aprender, empezar, estar, tener, terminar**)

Un abrazo desde España de tu amiga,

Diana

Nombre ______________________ Sección ______________ Fecha ____________

Actividad 23 **¿Qué hiciste?** Using complete sentences, answer the following questions about the last concert you saw.

1. ¿A quién viste? ______________________
2. ¿Con quién fuiste? ______________________
3. ¿A qué hora empezó? ______________________
4. ¿Cuándo terminó? ______________________
5. ¿Dónde se sentaron Uds.? ______________________
6. ¿Pudiste ver y oír bien? ______________________
7. ¿Cuánto te costó la entrada? ______________________
8. ¿Qué canciones (*songs*) tocaron? ______________________
9. ¿Cuál de las canciones fue tu favorita? ______________________

Actividad 24 **¿Cómo era?** Answer these questions about the same concert using complete sentences.

1. ¿Había mucha gente? ______________________
2. ¿Cuántos músicos (*musicians*) había? ______________________
3. ¿Qué ropa llevaban los músicos? ______________________
____
4. ¿Cómo era el escenario (*set*)? ______________________
____
5. ¿Cómo reaccionaba el público mientras escuchaba las canciones? ______________________
____
6. ¿Usaron efectos especiales (láser, video, etc.)? Si contestas que sí: ¿Qué hacían los músicos mientras Uds. veían los efectos especiales? ______________________
____
____
7. ¿Valió la pena ir al concierto o no? ¿Por qué sí o no? ______________________
____

Actividad 25 **Un concierto.** In order to describe an event well, you need to use the preterit and the imperfect. Use the information from *Actividad 23* and *Actividad 24* to write an email to a friend telling him/her about the concert you saw. Describe what you did, what happened, and what the concert was like. Add more details if needed.

_________________________:

____

____

____

____

____

____

____

____

____

____

____

____

Un abrazo,

____

Lectura

Estrategia de lectura: Activating Background Knowledge

You have already learned that by activating background knowledge prior to reading a text, you can increase your comprehension. In the following activities, you will have an opportunity not only to activate your background knowledge to become a better reader, but also to develop a greater sense of cultural understanding. By examining your knowledge of your own culture, you can better understand another one.

Actividad 26 **Aquí.** Craig, a Spanish teacher in the U.S., asked Diana to write to him in Spanish, with information about the education system in Spanish-speaking countries so that he could share it with his classes. Before reading Diana's email, answer these questions about universities in the U.S.

1. Para entrar a una universidad en los Estados Unidos, normalmente hay que tomar un examen de ingreso (*entry*). ¿Cómo se llama uno de los exámenes de ingreso?

   ____

2. ¿Es normal empezar estudios universitarios sin saber la especialización?

   ☐ Sí ☐ No

Continued on next page →

Nombre ______________________ Sección ______________ Fecha ____________

3. ¿Se pueden estudiar asignaturas en diferentes facultades (*departments or schools*)?

❒ Sí ❒ No

4. ¿Es común salir de la ciudad natal (*hometown*) para asistir a la universidad?

❒ Sí ❒ No

5. ¿Cuesta mucho o poco la educación universitaria en los Estados Unidos?

❒ Mucho ❒ Poco

Asunto: Sistema educativo

Querido Craig:

Recibí tu email hace unos días, pero no tuve tiempo para contestarte antes porque estaba ocupadísima con mis clases de literatura en la universidad. Por fin comencé mis vacaciones y ahora tengo tiempo para escribirte unas líneas. ¿Cómo estás? ¿Cómo va tu clase de español? ¿Mucho trabajo?

En tu email me pides información sobre el sistema educativo hispano para usar en tu clase de español. Bueno, a nivel universitario los estudiantes deben pasar primero un examen para entrar en la universidad, pero desde el momento en que entran comienzan a especializarse. Por ejemplo, si quieres estudiar psicología, entras en esa facultad (lo que nosotros llamamos *department*) y estudias asignaturas de ese campo desde el primer día, no como en los Estados Unidos, donde tomas asignaturas de varios campos. Aquí los estudiantes tienen una preparación más global en la escuela secundaria. Y por lo que me contaron unos amigos, el sistema de educación superior es parecido al de España en casi toda Hispanoamérica.

En general, la gente va a la universidad en el lugar donde vive y no se muda a otra parte del país. Aunque muchas ciudades grandes tienen ciudades universitarias, en otras, las diferentes facultades están en distintas partes de la ciudad. Esto no es ningún problema porque en general solo necesitas ir a una facultad. ¡Y el tamaño de algunas de estas universidades! ¡Una sola facultad puede tener alrededor de veinte mil estudiantes! Increíble, ¿no? Algunas universidades importantes son la Central en Venezuela, la Universidad de Costa Rica, la Complutense de Madrid, y, por supuesto, la UNAM en México con casi 300.000 estudiantes.

¿Qué más te puedo contar? ¡Ah, sí! La educación pública generalmente es gratis o cuesta poco; mejor dicho, los ciudadanos pagan impuestos que ayudan a mantener las universidades. En lugares como Cuba, por ejemplo, los estudiantes universitarios trabajan en el campo para devolver ese dinero al gobierno. También hay universidades donde sí tienes que pagar, pero es algo mínimo; yo, por ejemplo, pago 250 euros por año en la Complutense de Madrid. Naturalmente, también existen las universidades privadas donde los estudiantes pagan la matrícula, y a veces es cara.

Bueno, no se me ocurre qué más decirte sobre el sistema educativo universitario. Una cosa interesante aquí en la Complutense es que no todos los estudiantes pagan exactamente lo mismo, por ejemplo, un estudiante de medicina paga más que un estudiante de arte, y si tienes que repetir un curso, es más caro la segunda vez. Un amigo también me contó que en Colombia se paga según los ingresos de la familia, es decir que si un estudiante viene de una familia pobre, no paga nada.

Si tienes alguna pregunta, puedes mandarme otro email; por fin tengo acceso a una computadora. ¿No te gustaría venir a estudiar aquí? Para mí estas son circunstancias ideales: estoy aprendiendo cantidades, del idioma, de la cultura y de la gente; además, la comida española es deliciosa. Siempre pienso en ti cuando como paella. Tienes que venir a probarla.
Espero entonces noticias tuyas.

Un abrazo,

Diana

Actividad 27 **Allá.** In the first column, you will find some facts about the university system in the U.S. In the second column, write the corresponding information about universities in the Spanish-speaking world, according to the email.

Estados Unidos	El mundo hispano
1. Para entrar en la universidad, hay que tomar un examen de ingreso (SAT, ACT).	1. ______
2. Los estudiantes pueden pasar los primeros años de universidad sin saber su especialización.	2. ______
3. Los estudiantes pueden estudiar asignaturas en diferentes facultades.	3. ______
4. Muchos estudiantes no estudian en su pueblo o su ciudad; muchos estudian en otro estado.	4. ______
5. La educación universitaria cuesta un ojo de la cara.	5. ______
6. Todos los estudiantes pagan la misma matrícula.	6. ______

Nombre ______________________________ Sección ________________ Fecha ____________

Capítulo 9 Repaso

Saber and *conocer*

In Chapter 4, you studied when to use **saber** and **conocer.**

You use **saber** to say what someone *knows how to do* and to state factual information that someone *knows.*

> Ella **sabe** esquiar muy bien.
> Él **sabe** la dirección de mi casa y el número de teléfono.

You use **conocer** when saying that someone *knows a person* or *is familiar with a place or a thing.*

> Yo **conozco** a Jesús Covarrubias; es de Puerto Varas, Chile.
> **Conozco** Puerto Varas; es un pueblo muy bonito.

When **saber** and **conocer** are used in the preterit, they have a different meaning when translated into English. This is because the use of the preterit implies the beginning of an action. Study these examples and their explanations.

> Verónica me contó todo y así por fin **supe** la verdad.
> *Veronica told me everything and that's how I found out the truth. (The start of knowing something is to find it out.)*

> **Conocí** a Hernán en una fiesta en casa de mis amigos.
> *I met Hernán at a party at my friends' house. (The start of knowing someone is to meet him/her.)*

Actividad 1 **Conversaciones.** Complete the following conversations with the correct present, preterit, or imperfect form of **saber** or **conocer.**

1. —Por favor, señor, ¿____________________ Ud. dónde está la calle O'Higgins?

   —Lo siento, no ____________________ muy bien esta ciudad. ____________________ que está cerca de aquí, pero no ____________________ exactamente dónde.

2. —Juan ya ____________________ que Jorge iba a ir a Cochabamba este fin de semana con Paulina, pero no nos dijo nada.

   —Es verdad. ¿Cuándo lo ____________________ tú?

   —Cuando me lo dijo Paulina. ¿Y tú?

   —Lo ____________________ cuando Ricardo me lo dijo.

Continued on next page →

—¿Ricardo? Yo no ____________________ a ningún Ricardo. ¿De quién hablas?

—Trabaja en la agencia de viajes de la calle Libertador.

—Ah sí... Ricky. Lo ____________________ en un viaje que hice a Caracas.

3. —Oye Carmen, ¿____________________ qué autobús debo tomar para ir a la calle Ibiza?

—Lo siento, no ____________________ la calle Ibiza.

—Está cerca del Parque del Retiro.

—____________________ que el 62 pasa por allí.

—Gracias.

4. —¿Dónde ____________________ tu padre a tu madre?

—La ____________________ en un accidente de coche.

—¡¿De veras?!

—Él dice que los frenos no funcionaron y por eso chocó con el carro de mi madre.

—Bueno, todos nosotros ____________________ que tu padre no maneja bien... siempre tiene por lo menos un accidente al año.

Nombre ______________________ Sección ____________ Fecha __________

Capítulo 10 Mi casa es tu casa

Vocabulario esencial I

Los números ordinales

Actividad 1 **La primera actividad.** Completa cada oración con el número ordinal apropiado.

1. Ellos viven en el ________________ piso. (2)
2. Ricardo llegó en ________________ lugar. (3)
3. María fue la ________________ persona en recibir su dinero. (5)
4. Ana terminó ________________. (7)
5. Perú ganó el ________________ premio (*prize*). (4)
6. Carlos llegó ________________. (3)
7. Tengo que estudiar ________________; después puedo salir. (1)
8. Compraron un apartamento en el ________________ piso y pueden ver toda la ciudad. (9)
9. Guillermo fue el ________________ hijo de su familia que terminó la universidad. (1)
10. Esta es la ________________ oración. (10)

Actividad 2 **¿En qué piso?** Imagina que eres portero(a). Estos son los buzones (*mailboxes*) del edificio de apartamentos donde trabajas. Usando oraciones completas, contesta las preguntas que te hacen las visitas que van al edificio.

101 Martín	**301** Pascual	**501** Robles
201 Lerma	**401** Cano	**601** Fuentes

1. ¿En qué piso vive la familia Robles? ________________________________
____
2. ¿En qué piso vive Pepe Cano? ________________________________
____
3. ¿Sabe Ud. en qué piso viven los Srés. Martín? ________________________________
____
4. La Srta. Pascual vive en el sexto piso, ¿no? ________________________________
____

Las habitaciones de una casa

Actividad 3 **La casa.** Asocia las siguientes acciones con las habitaciones de una casa.

1. preparar comida ____________________
2. mirar la televisión ____________________
3. dormir ____________________
4. vestirse ____________________
5. llegar a casa ____________________
6. comer ____________________
7. afeitarse ____________________

Actividad 4 **¡Muchos gastos!** Cuando una persona alquila un apartamento tiene muchos gastos. Escribe a qué gasto se refiere cada una de las siguientes descripciones. Usa el artículo definido en tus respuestas.

1. El dinero que se paga cada mes por un apartamento. ____________________
2. El dinero extra que se paga antes de empezar a vivir en un apartamento.

   ____
3. Cuando usas computadoras o lámparas, tienes que pagar esto. ____________________
4. Cuando te bañas o te duchas, tienes que pagar esto. ____________________
5. Cuando preparas la comida, tienes que pagar esto. ____________________
6. Si hace mucho frío y quieres sentir calor tienes que pagar esto. ____________________

Gramática para la comunicación I

Using Affirmative and Negative Words

Actividad 5 **Negativos.** Completa las siguientes oraciones con **algún, alguno, alguna, algunos, algunas, ningún, ninguno o ninguna.**

1. No tengo ____________________ clase interesante.
2. —¿Cuántos estudiantes vinieron anoche?

   —No vino ____________________.
3. ¿Tienes ____________________ libro de economía?
4. —Necesitamos ____________________ discos compactos de salsa para la fiesta.

   —¿Discos compactos de salsa? Sí, creo que tengo ____________________.
5. —¿Tienes una tarjeta telefónica?

   —No, no tengo ____________________.

Continúa en la página siguiente →

Nombre ______________________ Sección ______________ Fecha __________

6. —¿Limpiaste todas las habitaciones?

   —No todas, pero limpié ______________________.

7. —¿Conoces ______________________ restaurante bueno cerca de aquí?

   —No hay ______________________ bueno, pero hay un restaurante muy barato.

Actividad 6 **El mensaje.** Completa este mensaje que Camila le escribió a su compañera de apartamento. Usa palabras afirmativas y negativas (**ningún, algún, ninguna,** etc.).

> Pilar:
>
> Busqué y no encontré ______________________ toalla. Si tienes tiempo, favor de lavarlas. Voy a ir al supermercado esta tarde para comprar ______________________ cosas; si quieres algo en especial, voy a estar en la oficina y no hay ______________________ problema, puedes llamarme allí. Otra cosa, iba a escuchar un disco compacto de los Gypsy Kings, pero no encontré ______________________. Sé que tenemos ______________________ discos compactos de ellos; ¿sabes dónde están?
>
> Camila
>
> P.D. Esta noche van a venir ______________________ amigos para estudiar.

Talking About the Unknown: The Present Subjunctive

Actividad 7 **Busco apartamento.** Miguel busca apartamento. Completa lo que dice con la forma correcta del subjuntivo de los verbos indicados.

1. Busco un apartamento que ______________________ cerca del trabajo. (estar)
2. No me gusta subir escaleras (*stairs*); por eso necesito un apartamento que ______________________ ascensor (*elevator*). (tener)
3. Necesito estudiar; por eso, busco un apartamento que ______________________ tranquilo. (ser)
4. Tengo muchas plantas. Quiero un apartamento que ______________________ balcón. (tener)
5. No tengo mucho dinero; por eso, busco un apartamento que ______________________ poco. (costar)

Actividad 8 **¿Subjuntivo o indicativo?** Completa las siguientes oraciones con la forma apropiada del indicativo o del subjuntivo de los verbos indicados.

1. Mi novio conoce a una secretaria que ______________________ noventa palabras por minuto. (escribir)
2. Quiero un novio que ______________________ inteligente. (ser)
3. Mi director necesita un recepcionista que ______________________ hablar italiano. (saber)
4. Voy a estar en un hotel que ______________________ cuatro piscinas. (tener)
5. Necesitamos un carro que ______________________ nuevo. (ser)
6. Quiero un esposo que ______________________ bien. (bailar)
7. No veo a nadie que nos ______________________ ayudar. (poder)
8. Necesito unas clases que no ______________________ antes de las 10. (empezar)
9. Tengo una profesora que no ______________________ exámenes. (dar)
10. Tenemos unos profesores que ______________________ bien las lecciones. (explicar)
11. Busco un trabajo que ______________________ bien. (pagar)
12. Necesito un vendedor que ______________________ en Caracas. (vivir)
13. No conozco a nadie que ______________________ un Mercedes Benz. (tener)
14. En la librería tienen unos libros de arte que ______________________ muy poco. (costar)
15. No hay ningún carro aquí que me ______________________. (gustar)

Actividad 9 **El apartamento perfecto.** El año que viene vas a buscar apartamento. Describe el apartamento ideal para ti: el número de habitaciones y cómo es, cuánto cuesta el apartamento, dónde está, etc.

Voy a buscar un apartamento que ____

____

____

____

____

Actividad 10 **Habitación libre.** Buscas un/a compañero/a de apartamento. Escribe un anuncio (*advertisement*) para describir a la persona perfecta.

Busco un/a compañero/a que ____

____

____

____

____

Nombre ______________________ Sección ______________ Fecha ____________

Actividad 11 **Una clase fácil.** Ya tienes varias clases difíciles para el próximo semestre, pero necesitas unos créditos más. Buscas la clase perfecta: interesante pero sin mucho trabajo. Tu compañero/a de habitación siempre encuentra clases "fáciles". Descríbele la clase que buscas.

Necesito una clase fácil con un profesor que ______________________________________

____

____

____

____

Un poco de todo

Actividad 12 **Los anuncios personales. Parte A:** Recibiste la siguiente nota de un amigo. Completa la nota con palabras afirmativas y negativas (**ningún, algún, ninguna,** etc.).

> Hola:
>
> Tengo un problema. Nunca conozco a
> ____________________ chica que quiera salir
> conmigo. Quiero escribir un anuncio personal.
> Escribí ____________________ líneas, pero no
> me salieron bien. De verdad no tengo
> ____________________ idea sobre qué escribir.
> ¿Por qué no me escribes el anuncio tú?
> Gracias,
>
> Miguel Ángel

Parte B: Como tú eres una persona cómica y escribes bien, vas a escribir un anuncio personal para tu amigo Miguel Ángel. Primero, describe cómo es él y qué le gusta hacer (indicativo). Luego, describe el tipo de mujer que busca (subjuntivo). Recuerda que estás escribiendo por él.

Yo ____

____

____

____

____

Vocabulario esencial II

En la casa

Actividad 13 **¿Dónde está...?** Escribe en qué habitación o habitaciones normalmente encuentras los siguientes muebles y electrodomésticos. Incluye el artículo definido.

1. sofá ______________________________
2. inodoro ______________________________
3. horno ______________________________
4. cama ______________________________
5. estante ______________________________
6. mesa y seis sillas ______________________________
7. lavabo ______________________________
8. nevera ______________________________
9. televisor ______________________________
10. congelador ______________________________
11. cómoda ______________________________
12. espejo ______________________________

Actividad 14 **Necesitamos...** Gonzalo acaba de alquilar un apartamento semiamueblado. Mira el dibujo y completa el mensaje que Gonzalo le escribió a su compañero de apartamento con los muebles y electrodomésticos apropiados.

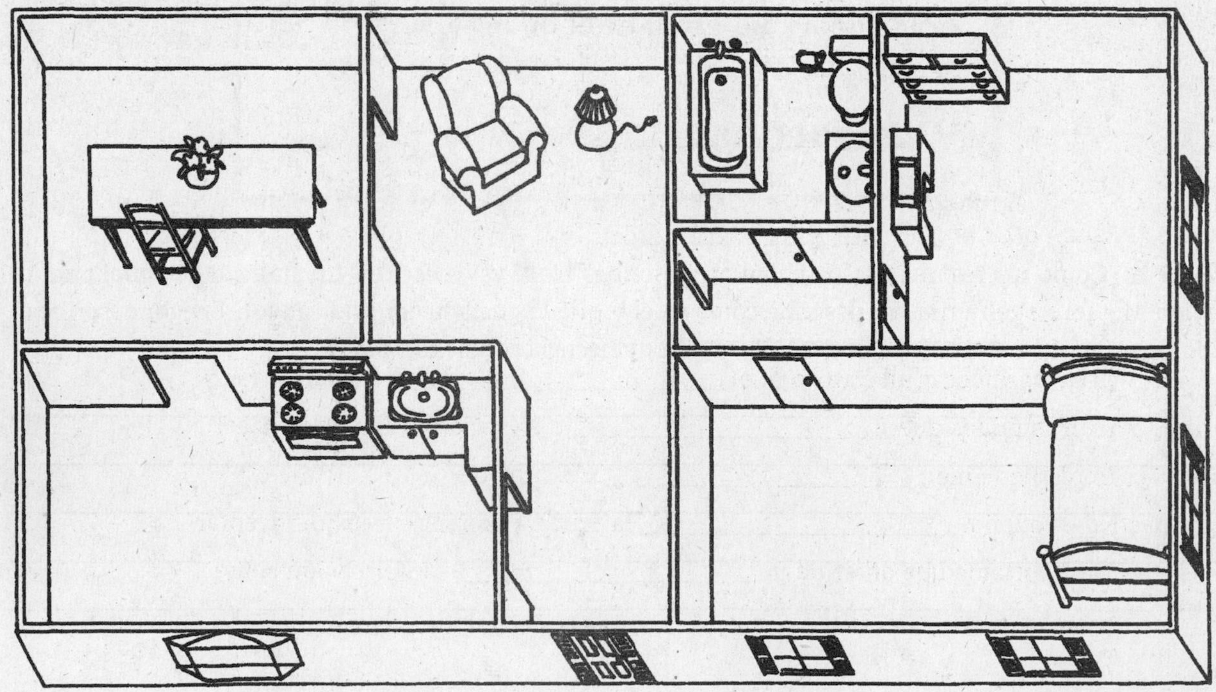

Continúa en la página siguiente →

Nombre ______________________ Sección ______________ Fecha ____________

Paco:

En la sala solo hay ________________________________;
entonces necesitamos ________________________________
________________________. *En el comedor* ________________
________________________.

Un dormitorio tiene ________________________________
y el otro ________________________________.
Por eso, necesitamos ________________________________.

Tenemos un problema enorme en la cocina: tenemos ________________
________________________________,
pero ________________________________.

Podemos hablar más esta noche.

Chau,

Gonzalo

Gramática para la comunicación II

Giving Advice and Stating Desires: Other Uses of the Subjunctive

Actividad 15 **La influencia.** Jaime quiere ir a vivir a California y sus amigas tienen muchos consejos para él. Completa la conversación con el infinitivo o la forma apropiada del subjuntivo de los verbos indicados.

ANA Te aconsejo que ______________ a Sacramento. (ir)

MARTA Quiero que nos ______________ una vez al mes. (llamar)

ANA Es importante que ______________ un carro nuevo antes del viaje. (comprar)

MARTA Es mejor ______________ por avión. (viajar)

ANA Necesitas buscar un trabajo que ______________ interesante. (ser)

MARTA Te prohibimos que ______________ a fumar otra vez. (comenzar)

ANA Te pido que me ______________. (escribir)

MARTA No es bueno ______________ la primera oferta de trabajo. (aceptar)

ANA Es importante que antes de ir, ______________ información sobre apartamentos. (tener)

Continúa en la página siguiente →

MARTA Espero que ______________________ fotos de tu apartamento nuevo. (sacar)

ANA Te recomiendo no ______________________ con cualquier (*any*) Fulano, Mengano y Zutano. (salir)

MARTA Es importantísimo que ______________________. (divertirse)

JAIME Bien, bien... ¿y si decido ir a Colorado?

Actividad 16 **Los tíos preguntones.** Magdalena pasó el día con sus tíos que son muy simpáticos, pero siempre le preguntan demasiado. Escribe lo que contestó Magdalena a sus preguntas, algunas discretas y otras indiscretas con el subjuntivo.

1. ¿Tus compañeros de apartamento quieren que cocines mucho?
   Sí, ____.
2. ¿Les prohíbes a tus compañeros que hagan fiestas?
   No, ____.
3. ¿Tus compañeras de apartamento y tú les prohíben a sus amigos que fumen en el apartamento?
   Sí, ____.
4. ¿Tu novio quiere que vivas con él?
   No, ____.
5. ¿Tus padres quieren que vivas en una residencia en vez de un apartamento?
   No, ____.
6. ¿Tus padres te aconsejan que cambies de especialización?
   No, ____.
7. ¿Tu profesor de francés te prohíbe que otros te ayuden con tus composiciones?
   Sí, ____.
8. ¿Tu profesor de francés les recomienda a Uds. que usen un CD-ROM?
   Sí, ____.
9. ¿Quieres que tu tío y yo vayamos a visitarte el mes que viene?
   No, ____.
10. ¿Quieres visitarnos durante tus próximas vacaciones?
    Sí, es buena idea que ____.

Nombre ______________________ Sección ______________ Fecha ____________

Actividad 17 **La queja.** Lee esta carta que escribió Raimundo Lerma a una agencia de protección al consumidor en Nicaragua. Luego, completa la respuesta de la agencia.

> Puerto Cabezas, 17 de abril de 2006
>
> Estimados señores:
>
> La semana pasada compré una tostadora. Funcionó por tres días y ahora no funciona. Busqué y no encontré ninguna garantía. Volví a la tienda para devolverla y recibir mi dinero, pero no me lo quisieron dar. Ahora tengo un problema: gasté 850 córdobas por una tostadora que no funciona. ¿Qué puedo hacer?
>
> Gracias por su atención,
>
> *Raimundo Lerma Zamora*

> Managua, 20 de abril de 2006
>
> Estimado Sr. Lerma:
>
> Le aconsejamos que ______________________________,
>
> pero es importante que ______________________________.
>
> Si todavía tiene problemas, es mejor que ______________________
>
> ____.
>
> Atentamente,
>
> *Susana Valencia Blanco*
>
> Susana Valencia Blanco
>
> Defensa del consumidor

Actividad 18 **Un problema serio.** Tu hermano menor tiene problemas con las drogas. Tus padres no saben qué hacer y te pidieron consejos. Completa las siguientes oraciones para ayudarlos.

1. Es mejor que Uds. ______________________________.
2. Les aconsejo que Uds. ______________________________.
3. Es bueno que Uds. no ______________________________.
4. Les pido que Uds. ______________________________.
5. Es importante que Uds. ______________________________.

Un poco de todo

Actividad 19 Ayuda. Hablas con dos estudiantes de Bolivia que llegaron hace poco a tu ciudad. Dales algunos consejos para ayudarlos a buscar un apartamento.

Tipo de apartamento

1. Deben buscar un apartamento que ______________________________

____

Precio de un alquiler típico

2. Un alquiler normal ______________________________

____

Depósito típico

3. Es típico pagar ______________________________

____

Buenas zonas de la ciudad para vivir

4. Les aconsejo que ______________________________

____

Actividad 20 El estudiante confuso. Lee el siguiente email de un estudiante de inglés que pide consejos a estudiantes que ya tomaron el curso. Luego, completa el email con consejos usando el infinitivo, el presente del indicativo o el presente del subjuntivo de los verbos indicados.

Asunto: Estudiante confuso

Queridos ex estudiantes de inglés elemental:

Tengo un pequeño problema. Me gusta mucho el inglés y estudio muchas horas la noche antes de los exámenes. Memorizo el vocabulario, leo las explicaciones gramaticales y hago toda la tarea en el cuaderno de ejercicios. En los primeros exámenes saqué buenas notas, pero en los últimos tres, mis notas fueron fatales. ¿Qué me aconsejan?

Estudiante confuso

Continúa en la página siguiente →

Nombre ______________________ Sección ______________ Fecha ____________

Asunto: Consejos

Querido estudiante confuso:

Primero, es bueno estudiar el inglés y es importante tener una actitud positiva. Tu problema es que esperas hasta el último momento para estudiar. Hay algunas cosas que ______________ (ser) fáciles de hacer. Te aconsejamos que ______________ (estudiar) un poco todos los días. Es mejor que ______________ (empezar) a estudiar el vocabulario el primer día de cada capítulo y que después lo ______________ (repasar) diez o quince minutos cada día. También debes ______________ (hacer) las actividades de Internet. A nosotros nos gustan mucho porque corregir las actividades en Internet es rápido y tienes la respuesta correcta en un segundo. Es importante ______________ (comenzar) con las actividades de vocabulario y gramática y ______________ (terminar) con las actividades de lectura (conversaciones y párrafos) que son más abiertas. También tienes que ______________ (hacer) la tarea todos los días y no esperar hasta el último día. Una cosa más: Tenemos amigos que ______________ (sacar) buenas notas y estudiamos con ellos; esto es una ayuda enorme. Es importante buscar gente que ______________ (querer) trabajar con otros y que ______________ (venir) preparada a colaborar.

Cuando estudias a última hora, recuerdas algunas cosas para el examen, pero después de dos días no sabes mucho. Por eso, es mejor ______________ (estudiar) un poco todos los días; así vas a recibir una buena nota en la clase y vas a poder hablar inglés bien. Esperamos que ______________ (sacar) una buena nota en la clase.

Un abrazo y buena suerte,

Ex estudiantes de inglés elemental

P.D. Es muy importante que ______________ (hablar) mucho en clase todos los días.

Lectura

Estrategia de lectura: Using the Dictionary

When you don't know what a word means, follow this procedure:

1. Skip it if it isn't important.
2. Discern meaning from context.
3. Check and see if the word is mentioned again in the reading.
4. Look it up in the dictionary.

Remember: The dictionary should be your last resort or you may become very frustrated trying to look up every single word you do not understand at first glance. See your textbook for information about how to use a dictionary.

Actividad 21 Cognados. Mientras lees el siguiente artículo sobre los mercados al aire libre, subraya (*underline*) los cognados.

LOS MERCADOS EN EL MUNDO HISPANO

Si viajas a un país hispano, un lugar interesante para visitar es el mercado al aire libre. Hay muchas clases de mercados: mercados de artesanía, de antigüedades, de comida y también de cosas en general. Algunos de estos mercados son principalmente para turistas y otros son para la gente del lugar. Vas a encontrar mercados que están abiertos todos los días y otros que solo abren días específicos.

En general, se pueden conseguir buenos precios en los mercados y, a veces inclusive, se puede regatear, pero tienes que tener cuidado con el regateo. En algunos lugares el regateo es común: el comerciante espera que el cliente no acepte el primer precio que se le dé, y que haga una contraoferta o pida un precio más bajo. Por otro lado, hay mercados donde no se regatea y si lo haces puedes insultar al comerciante. Para no meter la pata, es una buena idea ver qué hace la gente del lugar. Si ellos no regatean, pues entonces, es mejor no hacerlo.

Los mercados de artesanía y de comidas más conocidos de Hispanoamérica están en México, Guatemala y Perú. Allí prevalecieron las culturas azteca, maya e incaica y hoy día sus descendientes venden al público productos de la región y la artesanía que aprendieron a hacer de sus antepasados. En México, Guatemala y Perú están, por ejemplo, los mercados de Oaxaca, Chichicastenango y Huancayo respectivamente, donde la gente local vende telas típicas, hamacas, cerámica, especias y comidas. Para saber si los precios de las artesanías que tienen son buenos o no, y para comparar precios, es buena idea ir a las tiendas artesanales del gobierno, donde tienen productos similares.

En la ciudad de México y en Buenos Aires puedes encontrar mercados de antigüedades como la Lagunilla y el mercado de San Telmo, respectivamente. Allí es posible regatear. Los sábados y domingos son los días más interesantes porque hay mucha gente.

Para comprar de todo, existen mercados como el Rastro en Madrid, que está abierto todos los domingos. Este mercado es enorme y está dividido en diferentes zonas donde se venden cosas como antigüedades, ropa y artesanía moderna, y hay además una zona para comprar animales domésticos. En ese mercado normalmente no es apropiado regatear.

Si estás en un país hispano y quieres saber si hay mercados como los que se mencionan aquí, puedes averiguar en la oficina de turismo local o simplemente preguntarle a alguien del lugar.

Nombre ______________________ Sección ______________ Fecha ____________

Actividad 22 **Usa el diccionario.** Adivina qué significan las siguientes palabras del texto que acabas de leer. Luego, consulta el diccionario de abajo para ver si tus predicciones son ciertas.

	Guess	Dictionary Definition
1. línea 2: **artesanía**	______________	______________
2. línea 6: **conseguir**	______________	______________
3. línea 10: **meter la pata**	______________	______________
4. línea 13: **prevalecieron**	______________	______________
5. línea 16: **telas**	______________	______________

ar·te·sa·ní·a f. *(habilidad)* craftsmanship; *(producto)* crafts.
con·se·guir §64 tr. *(obtener)* to obtain; *(llegar a hacer)* to attain; *(lograr)* to manage.
pa·ta f. ZOOL. *(pie)* paw, foot; *(pierna)* leg; COLL. *(pierna humana)* leg; *(base)* leg <*las patas de la mesa* the legs of the table>; ORNITH. female duck ◆ **a cuatro patas** on all fours • **a p.** COLL. on foot • **estirar la p.** COLL. to kick the bucket • **meter la p.** COLL. to put one's foot in it • **p. de gallo** crowfoot.
pre·va·le·cer §17 intr. *(sobresalir)* to prevail; BOT. to take root.
te·la f. *(paño)* fabric; *(membrana)* membrane; *(nata)* film; *(de araña)* web; ANAT. film; BOT. skin; ARTS *(lienzo)* canvas; *(pintura)* painting ◆ **poner en t. de juicio** to call into question • **t. adhesiva** adhesive tape • **t. aislante** electrical tape • **t. metálica** wire netting.

Actividad 23 **Consejos para turistas.** Después de leer el artículo, explica qué aconseja el autor sobre estos temas:

1. el regateo ____
____
2. cómo saber si los precios son buenos o malos ______________________
____
3. cuándo ir a la Lagunilla y a San Telmo ______________________
____
4. si se puede regatear en el Rastro de Madrid ______________________
____

Nombre ______________________ Sección ______________ Fecha ____________

Capítulo 11 El tiempo libre

Vocabulario esencial I

Los pasatiempos

Actividad 1 **Asociaciones.** Escribe la letra del pasatiempo de la Columna B que mejor corresponda con la(s) palabra(s) de la Columna A.

A	B
1. _______ plantas	a. hacer crucigramas
2. _______ el póker	b. tejer
3. _______ hacer una blusa	c. hacer jardinería
4. _______ mecánico	d. jugar juegos de mesa
5. _______ preparar comida	e. coleccionar tarjetas de béisbol
6. _______ tres horizontal	f. jugar con juegos electrónicos
7. _______ hacer un suéter	g. navegar por Internet
8. _______ Pablo Picasso	h. cocinar
9. _______ PlayStation, Xbox	i. coser
10. _______ dinero	j. arreglar el carro
11. _______ Monopolio, Scrabble	k. coleccionar monedas
12. _______ conexión por cable, ADSL	l. jugar a las cartas
13. _______ Sammy Sosa, Manny Ramírez	m. pintar

Gramática para la comunicación I

Expressing Doubt and Certainty: Contrasting the Subjunctive and the Indicative

Actividad 2 Por las dudas. Completa las siguientes oraciones con la forma correcta del indicativo o del subjuntivo de los verbos indicados.

1. Dudo que Laura ______________________ mañana. (venir)
2. Es posible que él ______________________ crucigramas contigo. (hacer)
3. Es evidente que nosotros ______________________ un problema. (tener)
4. No es verdad que mi madre ______________________ mucho. (coser)
5. ¿Crees que Paco ______________________ mucho a las cartas? (jugar)
6. No creo que Raúl ______________________ arreglar el carro. (saber)
7. Es cierto que yo ______________________ hacerlo. (poder)
8. El médico cree que tú ______________________ comer menos. (deber)
9. Estamos seguros de que el profesor ______________________ buenas notas. (dar)
10. Es probable que ______________________ la carta hoy. (llegar)
11. Es verdad que Uds. ______________________ mucho. (pescar)
12. Quizás mis hermanos ______________________ venir esta noche. (querer)
13. Es obvio que la clase ______________________ a ser difícil. (ir)
14. Es cierto que tú ______________________ poesías preciosas. (escribir)
15. No crees que Jorge ______________________ aquí en Madrid, ¿verdad? (estar)
16. Tal vez yo ______________________ la lotería algún día. (ganar)
17. No hay duda que tu padre ______________________ bien. (bailar)
18. Está claro que ella nos ______________________. (mentir)
19. Es dudoso que nosotros ______________________ juegos de mesa hoy. (jugar)
20. ¿Crees que el profesor de historia me ______________________? (odiar)
21. No es verdad que los crucigramas ______________________ aburridos. (ser)

Actividad 3 Los pasatiempos. Parte A: Completa la siguiente encuesta (*survey*) sobre los pasatiempos. Luego, completa la encuesta otra vez, con las preferencias de uno de tus padres o de un(a) amigo(a). Escribe tus iniciales y las de la otra persona en la columna apropiada, según las preferencias.

Me/Le gusta:	**mucho**	**poco**	**nada**
1. navegar por Internet	______	______	______
2. pescar	______	______	______
3. hacer crucigramas	______	______	______

Continúa en la página siguiente →

4. jugar juegos de mesa ____________ ____________ ____________
5. coser ____________ ____________ ____________
6. jugar con videojuegos ____________ ____________ ____________
7. pintar ____________ ____________ ____________
8. arreglar carros ____________ ____________ ____________
9. jugar a las cartas ____________ ____________ ____________
10. jugar al billar ____________ ____________ ____________

Parte B: Ahora, escríbele una nota a la persona de la **Parte A.** Uds. van a pasar el fin de semana juntos. Recomienda actividades que les gusta hacer.

➤ ***Como a nosotros nos gusta arreglar carros, es posible que trabajemos en mi garaje. También, como siempre pintas, me puedes pintar...***

____

____

____

____

Actividad 4 **Tal vez...** Lee las siguientes conversaciones y contesta las preguntas, usando oraciones completas. Usa **tal vez** o **quizás** en tus respuestas.

➤ —¿Puedo ver uno de esos?
—Claro que sí.
—Es muy bonito. ¿Cuánto cuesta?
—Solo 295 euros.
¿Dónde están?
Tal vez estén en una tienda.
Quizás estén en una tienda.

1. —Necesito una carta más.
—¿Solo una? Vas a perder.
—Yo siempre gano.
¿Qué están haciendo? ______________________________

2. —Bienvenidos al programa. Hoy vamos a preparar una ensalada. Primero lavo y corto la lechuga, después lavo bien los tomates y también los corto, pero no muy pequeños...
¿Dónde está esta persona? ______________________________
¿A quiénes crees que les esté hablando? ______________________________

3. —¿Cómo que no me queda dinero?
—No señor, no hay nada.
—Pero, debo tener algo.
¿Dónde están? ______________________________

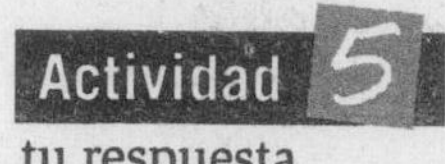 **Tu impresión.** Lee este mensaje que recibiste de tu amigo Ernesto. Luego, completa tu respuesta.

Hola:

Creo que tengo problemas con mi esposa, pero tal vez sea mi imaginación. Hace dos meses empezó un trabajo nuevo como arquitecta. Al principio todo iba bien, pero comenzó a trabajar con un arquitecto joven y últimamente está trabajando muchas horas (anoche no regresó a casa hasta las diez y media). Dice que le gusta mucho el trabajo y sé que, para ella, es muy importante trabajar. Dice que la semana que viene, ese arquitecto y ella tienen que ir a otra ciudad por dos días para asistir a una conferencia. Ella me dice que no pasa nada, pero yo tengo mis dudas. Anteayer, en vez de volver en autobús, él la trajo a casa.

Es posible que no sea nada, pero no estoy seguro. ¿Qué crees tú? ¿Qué debo hacer?

Ernesto

Querido Ernesto:

Es evidente que ______________________________. *Es posible que* ______________________________. *También dudo que* ______________________________. *Pero es cierto que* ______________________________. *Te aconsejo que* ______________________________ *porque estoy seguro(a) de que* ______________________________. *Te deseo mucha suerte.*

Un abrazo,

____

Nombre ______________________ Sección ______________ Fecha ____________

Saying How an Action Is Done: Adverbs Ending in *-mente*

Actividad 6 **¿Cómo?** Escribe oraciones, usando las siguientes palabras. Haz cambios y añade otras palabras si es necesario.

➤ yo / correr / rápido / clase ***Yo corro rápidamente a clase.***

1. general / ellas / estudiar / biblioteca ______________________

____

2. mi / hermanos / hablar / constante / teléfono ______________________

____

3. yo / saber / cantar / divino ______________________
4. ellos / jugar con videojuegos / continuo ______________________
5. nosotros / poder / encontrar / trabajo / Caracas / fácil ______________________

____

Un poco de todo

Actividad 7 **Un anuncio.** Lee este anuncio y contesta las preguntas.

¿QUIERES SER INSTRUCTORA DE AEROBICS?

Inscríbete en:

Guiesca

Tenemos el mejor sistema de enseñanza por medio de un programa activo, con intervención de profesores ampliamente capacitados dentro de un agradable ambiente.

Servicios que presta: Gimnasia aeróbica, Jazz, Pesas.

Fdo. Iglesias y Calderón
No. 50 Jardín Balbuena
15900 5 - 73 - 63 -78
Inscripción de la S.E.P. No. Reg. 88:056

1. Marca las actividades que se pueden hacer en Guiesca.
   - ❒ levantar pesas
   - ❒ nadar
   - ❒ hacer ejercicio
   - ❒ jugar al squash
2. ¿Crees que Guiesca busque personas que tengan experiencia? ¿Por qué sí o no?

____

3. ¿Crees que sea un gimnasio para hombres? ¿mujeres? ¿hombres y mujeres?

____

¿Por qué crees eso? ______________________

Vocabulario esencial II

El desayuno

Actividad 8 **La palabra que no pertenece.** Escoge la palabra que no pertenece al grupo.

1. fresas, mantequilla, naranja, manzana
2. yogur, salchicha, tocino, jamón
3. churros, medialuna, galleta, jugo
4. jugo, café, cereal, chocolate caliente
5. tostadas, revueltos, duros, fritos

La preparación de la comida

Actividad 9 **En la cocina.** Escribe las letras de todas las cosas de la Columna B que asocias con cada verbo de la Columna A. Escribe todas las respuestas posibles para cada verbo.

A	B
1. __________ freír	a. salchicha
2. __________ cortar	b. jamón
3. __________ añadir	c. cuchillo
4. __________ darle la vuelta	d. olla
5. __________ hervir	e. azúcar
6. __________ revolver	f. pan
	g. yogur
	h. huevos
	i. sartén
	j. mantequilla
	k. recipiente
	l. tocino

Nombre ______________________ Sección ______________ Fecha __________

Gramática para la comunicación II

Giving Instructions: The Passive *se*

Actividad 10 **Una receta.** Completa la siguiente receta con la forma correcta de los verbos indicados. Usa el **se** pasivo.

UNA TORTILLA ESPAÑOLA

Primero, ______________ cuatro patatas grandes en	*cortar*
trozos pequeños. Segundo, ______________ una cebolla.	*cortar*
Después ______________ aceite en una sartén a fuego	*poner*
alto. ______________ las patatas y la cebolla al aceite	*añadir*
caliente. Mientras ______________ las patatas y la cebolla,	*freír*
______________ cuatro huevos en un recipiente.	*revolver*
______________ sal a los huevos. Después,	*añadir*
______________ las patatas y la cebolla con los huevos y	*revolver*
______________ todos los ingredientes en la sartén. Después	*poner*
de unos minutos, ______________ la vuelta. Al final,	*darle*
______________ una tortilla deliciosa con un grupo de amigos.	*comer*

Actividad 11 **Una ensalada.** Tu amiga es un desastre en la cocina. Para ayudarla, le escribiste un mensaje explicándole cómo se prepara una ensalada. Completa la receta con las palabras apropiadas.

Primero se lava y ______ ______________ la lechuga. Después ______ ______________ y ______ ______________ los tomates. ______ ______________ la lechuga en el plato y ______ ______________ los tomates encima de la lechuga. También puedes ______________ una cebolla si quieres y ponerla encima de la lechuga. Como te gusta mucho el queso, te aconsejo que ______________ un poco encima de todo. Ahora, ______ ______________ aceite y vinagre (pero poco vinagre), después ______ ______________ sal (y pimienta si quieres). Finalmente ______ ______________ todo y se come.

Other Uses of *para* and *por*

Actividad 12 ***¿Para o por?*** Completa estas oraciones con **para** o **por**.

1. Le cambié mi radio __________ su chaqueta.
2. Anoche caminamos __________ la playa __________ varias horas.
3. __________ mí, el trabajo es muy aburrido.
4. Mañana Jaime sale __________ Punta del Este.

Continúa en la página siguiente →

5. Mañana tengo que ir al médico; por eso Victoria va a trabajar _____________ mí.
6. ¿Cuánto pagaste _____________ los churros?
7. Eran las tres cuando me llamaste _____________ teléfono.
8. Mis padres van en tren de Valencia a Madrid y van a pasar _____________ Albacete.
9. Debes mandar los documentos _____________ email.
10. _____________ Álvaro, las tortillas de su abuela son deliciosas.
11. Trabajé más horas de lo normal _____________ ganar un poco más de dinero.
12. Compré galletas, croissants y jugo _____________ el desayuno.

Expressing Emotions: More Uses of the Subjunctive

Actividad 13 **¡Qué emoción!** Completa estas oraciones con el infinitivo o la forma correcta del indicativo o del subjuntivo de los verbos indicados.

1. A Mercedes le sorprende que tú no _____________ más. (leer)
2. Es una pena que _____________ bombas atómicas. (haber)
3. Espero _____________ dinero del banco esta tarde. (sacar)
4. A mi madre le gusta que yo la _____________ con los crucigramas del periódico. (ayudar)
5. Mi padre espera que la universidad _____________ a mi hermano. (aceptar)
6. Me alegro de que tú _____________ aquí. (estar)
7. Sentimos no _____________ venir mañana. (poder)
8. Temo que mi novia me _____________. (mentir)
9. Es fantástico que a Guillermo le _____________ arreglar carros. (gustar)
10. Miguel espera que su compañero le _____________ un buen desayuno. (preparar)
11. Es una pena no _____________ tiempo hoy para jugar a las cartas. (tener)
12. Rogelio se sorprendió de _____________ a Roberto en su clase. (ver)
13. Tenemos miedo de que el examen _____________ difícil. (ser)
14. A mi hermana le molesta que yo _____________ su guitarra. (tocar)

Actividad 14 **¿Qué sientes?** Describe tus emociones y opiniones sobre tu universidad. Escribe sobre el presente o el futuro. No escribas sobre el pasado.

➤ Es bueno que la ***universidad tenga una biblioteca grande.***

1. Me sorprendo de que _____________________________.
2. Es fantástico que _____________________________.
3. Me molesta que _____________________________.
4. Es una pena que _____________________________.
5. Me alegro de que _____________________________.
6. Tengo miedo de que _____________________________.

Nombre ______________________ Sección ______________ Fecha ____________

Un poco de todo

Actividad 15 **Las mentes curiosas quieren saber.** Lee los siguientes titulares (*headlines*). Algunos son de periódicos respetables y algunos de periódicos sensacionalistas. Escribe tus reacciones, usando estas frases: **Me sorprendo de que..., No creo que..., Me alegro de que..., (No) Es posible que..., Creo que...,** etc.

1. Viajes a Marte en el año 2015. ______________________
2. Cumple 110 años y todavía hace artesanías. ______________________
3. Mujer de 72 años tiene bebé. ______________________
4. Nueva droga del Amazonas. ¿La cura del cáncer? ______________________
5. Niño de 6 años va a competir en las semifinales de un campeonato de ajedrez contra adultos. ______________________
6. Costa Rica tiene más profesores que policías y no tiene militares. ______________________
7. Cada año España tiene más turistas que habitantes. ______________________
8. La fruta del futuro: La *nanzana*, una combinación de una naranja y una manzana. ______________________

Lectura

Estrategia de lectura: Topic Sentences and Supporting Evidence

As you read, you need to focus your attention in order to understand the text. One way to do this is to locate the topic sentence (**oración principal**) in each paragraph. Once you have identified these, you can look for supporting information (**ideas de apoyo**).

Actividad 16 **Oración principal e ideas de apoyo.** Mientras lees el siguiente artículo, escribe las oraciones principales de los párrafos indicados y toma apuntes sobre las ideas de apoyo.

Párrafo 2: ______________________

Ideas de apoyo:

____

____

____

Continúa en la página siguiente →

Párrafo 3: ____

____

Ideas de apoyo:

____

____

____

Párrafo 4: ____

____

Ideas de apoyo:

____

____

____

____

Párrafo 5: ____

____

Ideas de apoyo:

____

____

____

____

____

Nombre ______________________ Sección ______________ Fecha ____________

CURIOSIDADES Y COSTUMBRES DEL MUNDO HISPANO

En algunos países hispanos se encuentran enigmas difíciles de comprender. Hay enigmas arqueológicos intrigantes que se están investigando, pero quizás nunca se encuentre una explicación para ellos. Por otro lado, hay fenómenos religiosos curiosos que tienen su origen en civilizaciones pasadas.

Las líneas de Nasca

Uno de los fenómenos arqueológicos inexplicables son los dibujos de Nasca, Perú. Allí, en la tierra, hay dibujos gigantescos de animales y flores que solo pueden verse en su totalidad desde el aire. También hay unas líneas muy derechas. Algunos dicen que tal vez sean pistas de aterrizaje[1] que se hicieron en la época prehistórica para visitantes extraterrestres.

Otro enigma que contradice toda lógica está en la Isla de Pascua, Chile. Allí, al lado del mar, hay unas cabezas enormes de piedra volcánica. Hay mucha controversia sobre el origen de estos monolitos, pero se cree que se construyeron unos cuatrocientos años antes de Cristo. Estas piedras pesan más de veinte toneladas[2] cada una y, hoy en día, todavía es inexplicable cómo una pequeña población pudo moverlas tantos kilómetros, desde el volcán hasta la costa. Hay gente que afirma que es un fenómeno sobrenatural.

En el mundo hispano no solo hay fenómenos arqueológicos fascinantes; existen también algunas costumbres religiosas que muestran aspectos únicos de la cultura. Una de estas costumbres es cómo usan la hoja de coca los indígenas de Bolivia y Perú. Ellos le ofrecen la coca a la diosa Pachamama para que ella les dé buena suerte; también mascan[3] la hoja de coca para combatir el hambre y el cansancio que causa la altitud. La hoja de coca se usa además en esa zona para predecir el futuro y para diagnosticar enfermedades.

Un fenómeno religioso que coexiste con el catolicismo es la santería, común en varios países del Caribe. Es de origen africano y consiste en la identificación de dioses africanos con santos cristianos. Cuando los españoles trajeron a los esclavos a América, los forzaron a adoptar el cristianismo, pero ellos no abandonaron totalmente su propia religión y el resultado fue una mezcla de las dos religiones. La santería que se practica hoy en día varía de país en país. En Cuba, por ejemplo, los orishas (dioses) corresponden a los santos cristianos: Babalú es el nombre de San Lázaro y es el protector de los enfermos; Changó, el dios del rayo[4], es Santa Bárbara. Hay símbolos especiales asociados con cada orisha y rituales para honrarlos.

Estos fenómenos arqueológicos y estas costumbres religiosas nos muestran varios aspectos de la cultura hispana. Conocer las costumbres propias de otras culturas nos ayuda a comprenderlas.

---

[1]**pistas...** *landing strips* [2]*toneladas métricas. Una tonelada métrica = 2204 libras* [3]*they chew* [4]*lightning*

Actividad 17 **Preguntas.** Contesta estas preguntas, usando oraciones completas.

1. ¿Crees que las líneas de Nasca sean para extraterrestres? ____________________

____

2. ¿Cuál es el fenómeno inexplicable de la Isla de Pascua? ____________________

____

3. ¿Para qué usan la coca los indígenas de Perú y Bolivia? ____________________

____

4. ¿Cuál es el origen de la santería? ____________________

____

5. ¿Conoces otros fenómenos inexplicables en otras partes del mundo? ¿Cuál o cuáles? ____________________

____

Nombre ______________________ Sección ______________ Fecha ____________

Capítulo 11 Repaso

Para and *por*

In Chapters 5 and 11 you studied different uses of the words **para** and **por.** Study these examples and then complete the conversations that follow.

—¿**Para** qué estudias?	—Estudio **para** ser médico/abogado/etc.
—Pero trabajas también, ¿no?	—Sí, trabajo **para** J. Crew.
—En J. Crew, ¿la ropa es cara?	—Sí y no, depende. Es posible pagar $30 o $100 **por** un suéter.
—¿Cómo supiste del trabajo?	—**Por** un anuncio.
—¿Lo leíste en un periódico?	—No, un amigo me lo mandó **por** email.
—¿**Para** qué trabajas?	—Trabajo **para** tener dinero, **para** poder salir con mis amigos y **para** pagar mis estudios.
—¿Cuándo trabajas?	—Trabajo **por** la tarde los lunes, los martes y los jueves.
—En tu opinión, ¿es bueno estudiar y trabajar?	—**Para** otras personas, no sé, pero **para** mí, sí. En la universidad aprendo mucho, pero en el trabajo también aprendo.
—Pero si estudias, ¿hay días que no puedes ir a trabajar?	—Claro, pero tengo un amigo en el trabajo. Si él no puede trabajar, yo trabajo **por** él, y si yo no puedo, él trabaja **por** mí.
—¿Cuántos años más vas a estar en la universidad?	—Voy a estar aquí **por** dos años más.
—¿Y después de terminar?	—Pienso viajar **por** Suramérica.
—¿Cuándo te vas **para** tu pueblo **para** visitar a tus padres?	—Me voy **para** mi pueblo pronto.
—¿Cuándo es tu próxima visita?	—Voy **para** Navidad.

Actividad 7 **Conversaciones.** Completa las siguientes conversaciones con **para** o **por.**

Dos estudiantes de francés hablan:

—¿Entiendes la tarea que nos dio la profesora hoy en la clase de francés?

—__________ (1) mí, la lección __________ (2) mañana es fácil, pero hay otras cosas que son problemáticas.

—__________ (3) los estudiantes de inglés, los verbos son fáciles.

—Los verbos en francés son difíciles __________ (4) mí.

Dos aficionados al fútbol hablan sobre un nuevo jugador:

—Ahora Jorge juega al fútbol __________ (5) los Huracanes.

—Juega solo __________ (6) tener dinero y __________ (7) ser famoso. No me gusta su actitud.

—A mí tampoco. Si Jorge está enfermo, Lorenzo juega __________ (8) él. ¿Sabías eso?

—Lorenzo es mejor jugador y él juega __________ (9) divertirse.

Dos personas hablan sobre el hermano de uno de ellos:

—¿Conoces a mi hermano Hernando?

—No, ¿cómo es?

—__________ (10) mis padres, es el hijo perfecto.

—¿Y eso?

—__________ (11) Hernando, la educación universitaria es muy importante. Él estudia __________ (12) ser maestro de niños pequeños. Tiene clases __________ (13) la mañana, trabaja __________ (14) la tarde __________ (15) una compañía internacional y estudia __________ (16) la noche. Los lunes, los miércoles y los sábados corre __________ (17) el parque __________ (18) hacer ejercicio. Los domingos Hernando sale de la ciudad y se va __________ (19) el pueblo __________ (20) visitar a nuestros padres. Normalmente los visita __________ (21) un par de horas. Después, al volver a casa pasa __________ (22) la casa de nuestra abuela __________ (23) ver si está bien.

—Ya veo. ¿El señor perfecto tiene novia?

—Claro. Ella vive en otra ciudad, entonces él siempre le manda regalos pequeños. Y también le manda mensajes todos los días __________ (24) correo electrónico.

—Tienes razón, su vida es perfecta.

—No, perdón. __________ (25) mí, esa no es una vida perfecta. No puede ir a caminar __________ (26) la calle todas las noches con su novia, no puede verla, solo puede hablar con ella __________ (27) teléfono o mandarle mensajes __________ (28) correo electrónico.

—Tu hermano piensa en su futuro y tú piensas en el presente.

—Sí, es verdad. Hablando del presente, ¿por qué no nos vamos __________ (29) el club?

—Bueno, pero primero podemos pasar __________ (30) un cajero automático; necesito sacar dinero.

—Bien.

Nombre ______________________________ Sección ________________ Fecha ____________

Capítulo 12 ¡Viva la música!

Vocabulario esencial I

El correo y la red

Actividad 1 **Mandar una carta.** Escribe las palabras que corresponden a las siguientes cosas. Incluye el artículo definido en tus respuestas.

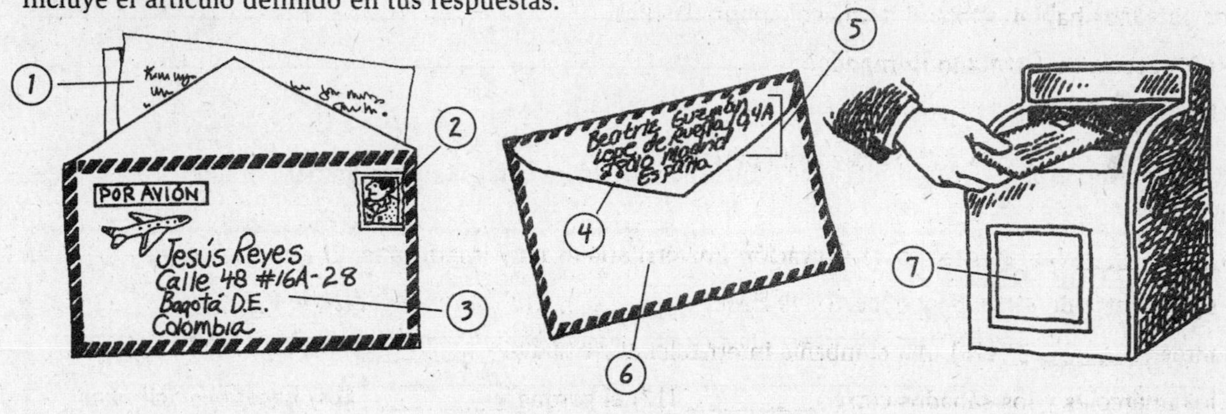

1. ______________________________
2. ______________________________
3. ______________________________
4. ______________________________
5. ______________________________
6. ______________________________
7. ______________________________

Actividad 2 **La red.** Combina las cosas de la Columna A con las de la Columna B.

A	B
1. ________ @	a. iTunes
2. ________ /	b. dos puntos
3. ________ :	c. Google
4. ________ enlace	d. arroba
5. ________ dirección de correo electrónico	e. dto2mo2@gmail.com
6. ________ buscador	f. dto2mo2
7. ________ bajar música	g. barra
8. ________ nombre de usuario	h. http://www.latinolink.com

Actividad 3 **El paquete. Parte A.** Estás en México y tienes que mandarle un paquete muy importante a tu jefe, Diego Velazco Ramírez. El paquete contiene unos contratos y lo vas a mandar al Hotel Meliá Castilla, Capitán Haya 43, 28020 Madrid, España. Es necesario que el paquete llegue mañana o pasado mañana. Completa la conversación que tienes con el empleado del correo.

EMPLEADO ¿Qué desea?

TÚ ______________________________

EMPLEADO ¿Adónde va el paquete?

TÚ ______________________________

EMPLEADO ¿Contiene comida o alcohol?

TÚ ______________________________

EMPLEADO ¿Cómo lo quiere mandar? ¿Por avión? ¿Urgente?

TÚ ______________________________

¿______________________________?

EMPLEADO Mañana o pasado mañana.

TÚ ______________________________

¿______________________________?

EMPLEADO 140,00 pesos. Favor de completar el formulario.

Parte B. Ahora, llena el formulario de aduanas. Puedes inventar la dirección del remitente.

ADUANA DE MÉXICO

Destinatario: ______________________________

____

____

Remitente: ______________________________

____

____

Contenido del paquete: ______________________________

____

____

Nombre ______________________ Sección ______________ Fecha ___________

Gramática para la comunicación I

Making Comparisons

Actividad 4 **Comparaciones.** Escribe oraciones comparando estas personas o cosas. ¡Ojo! Algunas usan superlativos y otras usan comparativos.

➤ Paris Hilton / Rosie O'Donnell / Oprah / delgado
Paris Hilton es la más delgada de las tres.

1. Danny DeVito / Tom Hanks / bajo ______________________
2. México / Guatemala / El Salvador / grande ______________________
3. el tango / la salsa / sensual ______________________
4. carro / costar / más / diez mil dólares ______________________
5. George W. Bush / Bill Clinton / George Bush / joven ______________________
6. el jazz / el merengue / el rock / bueno ______________________

Actividad 5 **El ejercicio y la salud.** Compara los siguientes gimnasios. Usa el comparativo o el superlativo.

	Cuerposano	Musculín	Barriguita
Número de clases aeróbicas	14/semana	7/semana	21/semana
Precio	$1.700/año	$2.500/año	$1.875/año
Piscina	50 metros	25 metros	40 metros
Número de miembros	1500 Hombres y mujeres	1400 Para toda la familia	1350 Solo mujeres
Extras	Bar con jugos y sándwiches	Máquinas de Coca-Cola, boutique	Bar, cafetería y restaurante

1. clases aeróbicas: Cuerposano / Musculín ______________________
2. precio: Cuerposano / Musculín / Barriguita ______________________
3. piscina: Cuerposano / Musculín / Barriguita ______________________

Continúa en la página siguiente →

4. número de miembros: Musculín / Barriguita ______________________________

____

5. En tu opinión, ¿cuál es el mejor gimnasio? ¿Por qué? ____________________

____

Actividad 6 **Los hermanos Villa.** Mira el dibujo de los hermanos Villa y lee las pistas (*clues*). Después identifica el nombre de la persona en cada dibujo, su edad y qué hace.

1 2 3 4 5

Pistas

Felisa es la más alta de las hermanas.

El estudiante tiene un año más que el músico y un año menos que la secretaria.

La secretaria tiene el pelo más largo de todos.

David es más alto que el músico.

El menor de la familia tiene veinticinco años y se llama Felipe.

La persona que tiene dos años más que Felisa es doctora.

El estudiante no trabaja.

La mayor de todos los hermanos tiene treinta y cuatro años y es la más delgada.

La hermana más alta de las tres es arquitecta.

Maribel es mayor que Ana; Ana tiene solo veintisiete años.

	Nombre	Edad	Ocupación
1.			
2.			
3.			
4.			
5.			

Actividad 7 **¿Cómo es tu familia?** Escribe una pequeña descripción de tu familia usando comparativos y superlativos. Usa adjetivos como **interesante, inteligente, trabajador/a, mayor, menor,** etc.

____

____

____

____

____

____

____

Nombre ______________________ Sección ______________ Fecha ______________

Making Requests and Giving Commands: Commands with *usted* and *ustedes*

Actividad 8 **Lo que deben hacer.** Lee estas recomendaciones que se pueden escuchar en una oficina de correos y luego cámbialas a órdenes de **Ud.** y **Uds.** Usa pronombres de complemento directo e indirecto si es posible.

➤ Ud. tiene que comprar las estampillas allí. ***Cómprelas allí.***

1. Deben hablar con el supervisor. ______________________
2. No debe beber Coca-Cola aquí. ______________________
3. Deben sentarse allí. ______________________
4. No pueden tocar la guitarra aquí. ______________________
5. Ud. tiene que explicarle su problema a mi supervisor. ______________________
6. Uds. deben mandarle el paquete a su madre por avión. ______________________
7. Señor, no puede poner los pies en la silla. ______________________
8. Aquí no pueden fumar. ______________________
9. Debe pagar allí. ______________________
10. Señores, el paquete está roto, tienen que arreglarlo antes de mandarlo. ______________________
11. Está cerrado. Deben volver mañana. ______________________

Actividad 9 **¡Ojo!** Mira estos dibujos y escribe órdenes apropiadas. Usa pronombres de complemento directo cuando sea posible.

1.

2.

3.

4.

1. ______________________
2. ______________________
3. ______________________
4. ______________________

Actividad 10 **Sin supervisión.** Los padres de Fabiana y Raúl se fueron de viaje a otra ciudad por el fin de semana. La madre les dejó un mensaje para recordarles lo que deben y no deben hacer. Completa el mensaje con las órdenes apropiadas de los verbos indicados.

Ya saben; vamos a quedarnos en el Hilton en Cartagena. Si necesitan algo, ________________ (llamarnos) al hotel. En la nevera hay una sopa de verduras y unos filetes. ________________ (Prepararlos) en una sartén grande con un poco de aceite. Por la noche, ________________ (salir) pero ________________ (regresar) a casa antes de las dos. No ________________ (olvidar) que tienen tarea para el lunes; ________________ (empezarla) temprano. Si quieren, ________________ (usar) la computadora de su padre. ________________ (Navegar) por Internet, pero no ________________ (bajar) música ni ________________ (visitar) salones de chat.

Mamá

P.D. Por supuesto, no ________________ (organizar) fiestas en la casa.

Actividad 11 **En la clase. Parte A:** Escribe dos órdenes que un/a profesor/a normalmente les dice a los estudiantes de español elemental antes de un examen final.

1. ____
2. ____

Parte B: Ahora, tú tienes la oportunidad de decirle algunas cosas al/a la profesor/a de español elemental. Escribe dos órdenes que le dirías *(would say)* antes del examen final. Usa la forma de Ud.

1. ____
2. ____

Un poco de todo

Actividad 12 **Instrucciones.** Termina las siguientes instrucciones que les dio una profesora a sus estudiantes. Usa los verbos indicados para escribir sus órdenes y luego comparativos para completar cada instrucción.

1. No ______________ (bajar) canciones de Internet en las computadoras de la universidad. Hoy día un CD es ______________ barato que ______________________________.
2. Todos saben su nombre de usuario. ________________ (Escribirlo) en un lugar seguro y luego

Continúa en la página siguiente →

________ (memorizar) la contraseña. Su contraseña es secreta, no ________ (dársela) a nadie o pueden tener ________ problemas que ______________________________________.

3. Para el trabajo que tienen que hacer, ____________ (buscar) información en la biblioteca. Los libros son ________ informativos ________ algunas páginas de Internet.
4. Al escribir el trabajo, ____________ (ser) creativos. Uds. tienen ________ ideas que ______________________________________.
5. Tienen que entregarme el trabajo terminado para el viernes a las 4:00 de la tarde. Como muchos de Uds. no van a estar el viernes porque van al museo con la clase de arte, ____________ (mandármelo) por email porque el correo eléctronico es ________ rápido que ______________________________________.

Vocabulario esencial II

La geografía

Actividad 13 **La variedad geográfica.** Asocia las palabras de la Columna A con los términos geográficos de la Columna B.

A		B
1.	________ Misisipí, Amazonas, Ebro	a. islas
2.	________ Caracas, Quito	b. desiertos
3.	________ Etna, Osorno y Popocatépetl	c. colina
4.	________ las Galápagos, Puerto Rico y Cuba	d. playas
5.	________ los Pirineos, los Andes	e. ríos
6.	________ Jack y Jill	f. océanos
7.	________ Atlántico, Pacífico	g. ciudades
8.	________ Malibú, Luquillo	h. lagos
9.	________ Michigan, Superior y Titicaca	i. montañas
10.	________ Sahara, Atacama	j. volcanes

Actividad 14 **La geografía.** Completa este crucigrama.

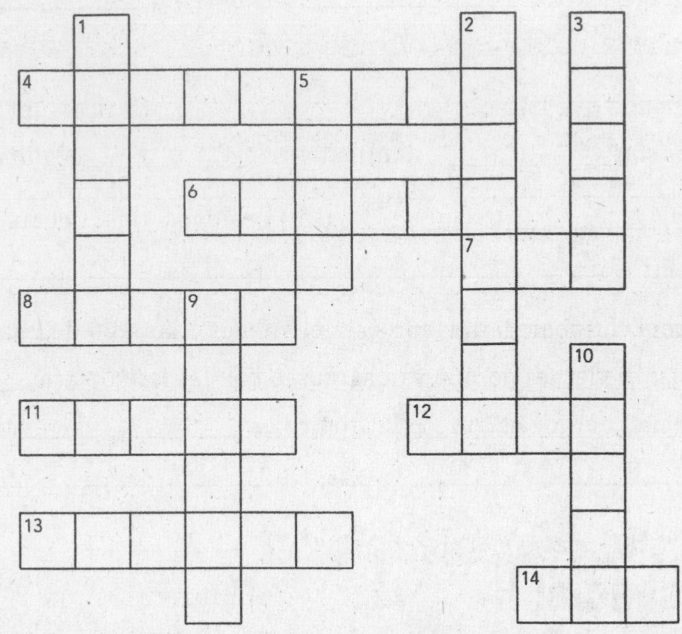

Horizontales

4. Es una carretera para vehículos de alta velocidad.
6. Es más pequeña que una montaña.
7. El Amazonas o el Orinoco.
8. Donde vive Tarzán.
11. Un lugar entre dos montañas: Napa es un ______.
12. Titicaca es el ______ navegable más alto del mundo.
13. El Atlántico o el Pacífico.
14. El Mediterráneo.

Verticales

1. Los romanos construyeron muchos, pero uno muy famoso y moderno conecta Manhattan y Brooklyn.
2. Iguazú o el salto Ángel.
3. No es la ciudad.
5. Puerto Rico, Cuba o Mallorca.
9. De esto sale lava cuando hace erupción.
10. Viajando por la ______ este de España, vimos el Mediterráneo.

Actividad 15 **Alquiler de carros.** Lee este anuncio de Hertz y contesta las preguntas usando oraciones completas.

Latinoamérica A Su Alcance[MR] con Hertz.

Descubra el colorido de un mundo de culturas.

Argentina. Brasil. Chile. Venezuela. Perú. Panamá. Y otros siete destinos en Latinoamérica. En cada uno encontrará un mundo de culturas. Países donde verá ruinas arqueológicas casi junto a modernas ciudades. Además de magníficas playas, paisajes montañosos, selvas y miles de maravillas naturales.

Desde Centroamérica hasta la Patagonia, Hertz le espera con un flamante auto, limpio y cómodo, con tarifas garantizadas en dólares (US$). Hertz le proporcionará el placer de descubrir las bellezas de este Nuevo Mundo, mientras disfruta del servicio y la experiencia de la compañía de alquiler de autos más importante en Latinoamérica.

Continúa en la página siguiente →

Nombre ______________________ Sección ______________ Fecha ____________

1. ¿En cuántos países latinoamericanos tiene oficinas Hertz? ______________________

2. Latinoamérica es un lugar de contrastes. ¿Con qué contrasta Hertz las ruinas arqueológicas?
____

3. Hertz habla de variedad geográfica. ¿Qué cosas menciona el anuncio? ______________________

4. ¿Dónde crees que esté la Patagonia? ¿Cerca o lejos de Centroamérica? ______________________

5. ¿Hertz te puede garantizar un precio antes de salir de los Estados Unidos o depende del país y del precio del dólar? ______________________

Gramática para la comunicación II

Making Comparisons: Comparisons of Equality

Actividad 16 **Comparaciones.** Escribe comparaciones basadas en los dibujos.

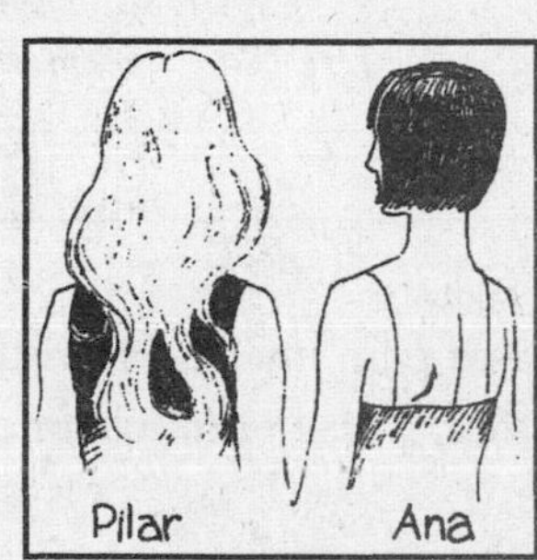

1. Isabel / Paco / alto ______________________
2. pelo / Pilar / Ana / largo ______________________
3. Paula / María / bonito ______________________
4. Pedro / Martín / dinero ______________________
5. Pepe / Laura / sueño ______________________
6. ojos / Elisa / Juana / pequeño ______________________

Actividad 17 **¿Idénticos?** Mario y David son dos hombres muy parecidos (*similar*). Escribe solo lo que tienen en común, usando **tan, tanto, tantos** o **tantas.**

	Mario	**David**
altura	1'80	1'80
hermanos	1	0
hermanas	3	3
carros	1	1
novias	2	1
coeficiente intelectual (IQ)	146	146
trabajos	2	3
sueldo	698 euros/semana	698 euros/semana
relojes Rólex	3	2
teléfonos celulares	2	1
llamadas recibidas por día	16	16

1. ______________________________
2. ______________________________
3. ______________________________
4. ______________________________
5. ______________________________
6. ______________________________

Actividad 18 **Los anuncios.** Trabajas para una compañía de publicidad. Tienes que escribir frases que llamen la atención (*catchy phrases*). Usa **tan... como** en tus oraciones.

➤ el detergente Mimosil
El detergente Mimosil te deja la ropa tan blanca como la nieve.

1. la película *Spiderman VI* ______________________________
____
2. el buscador Google ______________________________
____
3. la dieta Kitakilos ______________________________
____
4. el nuevo carro Mercedes Sport ______________________________
____

Nombre ______________________ Sección ______________ Fecha __________

Making Requests and Giving Commands: Commands with *tú*

Actividad 19 **Una vida de perros.** Tienes un perro inteligente pero a veces es malo. Escribe órdenes para tu perro.

1. sentarse ______________________
2. traerme el periódico ______________________
3. bailar ______________________
4. no molestar a la gente ______________________
5. no subirse al sofá ______________________
6. acostarse ______________________
7. hacerse el muerto ______________________
8. no comer eso ______________________
9. quedarse allí ______________________
10. venir aquí ______________________

Actividad 20 **Consejos para tu hermano.** Tu hermano menor va a comenzar sus estudios universitarios este año. Piensa tomar italiano elemental y, como estudias español, él te pidió consejos. Escríbele tus consejos usando órdenes e incluye otras palabras si es necesario.

1. llegar / clase / a tiempo ______________________
2. ir / oficina del profesor / si necesitar ayuda ______________________
   ____
3. no / salir / noche / antes / examen ______________________
4. no / copiar / respuestas / cuaderno de ejercicios ______________________
   ____
5. usar / CD-ROM / frecuentemente ______________________
6. tener / actitud positiva ______________________
7. no / entregar / tarea / tarde ______________________
8. no / dormirse / en clase ______________________
9. ser / estudiante bueno ______________________
10. decirle / al profesor / si no entender ______________________

Actividad 21 **Ayuda tecnológica.** La abuela de Alejandra no sabe mucho de computadoras, pero quiere aprender a ver fotografías que recibe en email y cómo mandarles fotos a otros amigos. Termina esta conversación entre Alejandra y su abuela. Usa órdenes de **tú** y pronombres de complementos directos e indirectos si es posible.

ABUELA Para abrir una foto de un email, hago clic aquí, ¿no?

ALEJANDRA Sí, abuela, ______________________.

Continúa en la página siguiente →

ABUELA Lo hice. Ahhh, ¡qué bonita! ¿La bajo ahora?

ALEJANDRA No, no ______________________. Solo vas a bajarla si quieres tener la foto para siempre en tu computadora.

ABUELA Huy, primero tengo que copiarla, ¿no?

ALEJANDRA Sí, ______________________.

ABUELA ¿Ahora abro un email nuevo?

ALEJANDRA Sí, ______________________ ahora.

ABUELA ¿Escribo la dirección y el mensaje?

ALEJANDRA Correcto, ______________________ ahora.

ABUELA ¿Y dónde copio la foto?

ALEJANDRA ______________________ allí mismo en el email después de lo que escribiste.

ABUELA ¡Huy! Aquí está. ¿Luego le mando el email a mi amigo?

ALEJANDRA Exacto. ______________________ ahora mismo.

ABUELA Tengo una nieta súper inteligente y muy buena profesora.

Un poco de todo

Actividad 22 **¿Cuánto sabes?** Marca estas oraciones con **C** (cierta) o **F** (falsa). Corrige las oraciones falsas.

1. _______ El Aconcagua es la montaña más alta del mundo.

____

2. _______ Hay más de veinticinco países de habla española en el mundo.

____

3. _______ San Agustín, en la Florida, es una ciudad tan vieja como Plymouth, Massachusetts, en los Estados Unidos.

____

4. _______ El salto Ángel, en Venezuela, es la catarata más alta del mundo.

____

5. _______ La papa es tan importante en Centroamérica y en México como el maíz en los Andes en Suramérica.

____

6. _______ Carlos Gardel fue el cantante de salsa más famoso del mundo.

____

7. _______ Las montañas de los Andes son tan altas como las Rocosas en Norteamérica.

____

Nombre ______________________________ Sección ________________ Fecha ____________

Actividad 23 **Imágenes satelitales.** Un profesor chileno le explica a su clase de segundo grado cómo mirar imágenes satelitales de su ciudad, Santiago, en Google. Escribe órdenes formales o informales.

PROFESOR ¿Todos están en la página Web de mapas de Google?

ESTUDIANTES Sí.

PROFESOR Bien. Ahora ________________ (mirar) el mapa, ________________ (buscar) la palabra "satélite".

PEPITO ¿Dónde la busco?

PROFESOR ________________ (buscarla) arriba a la derecha en el mapa.

PEPITO Gracias, ahora la veo.

PROFESOR Bueno, ahora ________________ (hacer) Uds. clic en la palabra "satélite". Una vez que hicieron esto, ________________ (escribir) "Santiago, Chile" y ________________ (hacer) clic en el botón que dice "búsqueda".

ESTUDIANTES ¡Qué bonito! ¡Increíble!

PEPITO Yo no veo fotos.

PROFESOR A ver Pepito, ¿hiciste clic?

PEPITO Ah, no señor.

PROFESOR Pues, ________________ (hacerlo) ahora.

PEPITO Ya veo.

PROFESOR Bien. Es posible ver la foto de Santiago desde más cerca o más lejos. ¿Ven esta línea vertical a la izquierda de la foto? ________________ (hacer) clic, pero no ________________ (levantar) el dedo, y luego ________________ (subir) o ________________ (bajar) el rectángulo. Si lo suben, van a ver la foto más de cerca.

ESTUDIANTES ¡No lo puedo creer! ¡Allí está mi casa! ¡Veo la escuela! ¡Allí está la piscina de mi casa!

ALICIA Mi computadora no funciona. Lo subo y lo bajo y no pasa nada.

PROFESOR Es que levantaste el dedo. ________________ (hacer) clic sin levantar el dedo. No ________________ (levantarlo). Ahora ________________ (subirlo) y ________________ (bajarlo).

ALICIA Ah, ya veo. Gracias.

Actividad 24 **El entrenador personal.** Carlos tiene que bajar de peso rápidamente antes de una operación y, por eso, va a un gimnasio todos los días con un entrenador personal. Termina estas instrucciones que le dio el entrenador a Carlos. Usa órdenes de **tú** de los verbos indicados y comparativos para completar los otros espacios en blanco.

1. ______________ (correr) 300 metros. Debes correr ______________ rápido como ______________ ____.

2. ______________ (sentarte) en esta silla. ______________ (levantar) la pierna derecha. No ______________ (bajarla). La pierna debe estar ______________ recta (*straight*) como ______________________. Después de un minuto ______________ (hacer) lo mismo con la izquierda.

3. Después de salir del gimnasio, no ______________ (ir) a MacDonalds y no ______________ (comer) comida alta en calorías. Si haces ejercicio y si comes bien, después de tu operación vas a recuperarte tan rápido ______________ un abrir y cerrar de ojos.

Lectura

Estrategia de lectura: Reading an Interview Article

Prior to reading an interview article, you should go through the following steps to give you some background information:

- Read the headline and subheadline.
- Look at accompanying photographs, drawings, graphs, or tables.
- Scan the text for the interviewer's questions.

Actividad 25 **Lee y adivina.** Lee el título, el subtítulo y las preguntas; luego mira los dibujos. Ahora, contesta esta pregunta.

¿Cuál es la idea principal del artículo?

a. la música de España
b. la historia de la música hispana
c. la historia de la música hispanoamericana

Continúa en la página siguiente →

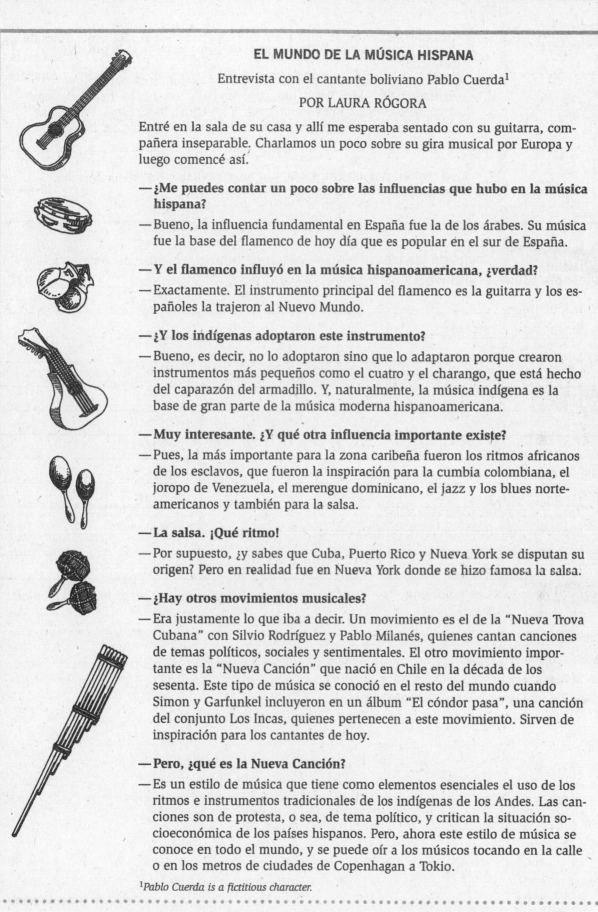

Nombre ______________________ Sección ______________ Fecha ____________

EL MUNDO DE LA MÚSICA HISPANA

Entrevista con el cantante boliviano Pablo Cuerda[1]

POR LAURA RÓGORA

Entré en la sala de su casa y allí me esperaba sentado con su guitarra, compañera inseparable. Charlamos un poco sobre su gira musical por Europa y luego comencé así.

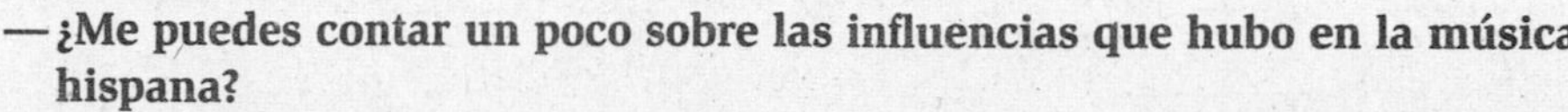

—¿Me puedes contar un poco sobre las influencias que hubo en la música hispana?

—Bueno, la influencia fundamental en España fue la de los árabes. Su música fue la base del flamenco de hoy día que es popular en el sur de España.

—Y el flamenco influyó en la música hispanoamericana, ¿verdad?

—Exactamente. El instrumento principal del flamenco es la guitarra y los españoles la trajeron al Nuevo Mundo.

—¿Y los indígenas adoptaron este instrumento?

—Bueno, es decir, no lo adoptaron sino que lo adaptaron porque crearon instrumentos más pequeños como el cuatro y el charango, que está hecho del caparazón del armadillo. Y, naturalmente, la música indígena es la base de gran parte de la música moderna hispanoamericana.

—Muy interesante. ¿Y qué otra influencia importante existe?

—Pues, la más importante para la zona caribeña fueron los ritmos africanos de los esclavos, que fueron la inspiración para la cumbia colombiana, el joropo de Venezuela, el merengue dominicano, el jazz y los blues norteamericanos y también para la salsa.

—La salsa. ¡Qué ritmo!

—Por supuesto, ¿y sabes que Cuba, Puerto Rico y Nueva York se disputan su origen? Pero en realidad fue en Nueva York donde se hizo famosa la salsa.

—¿Hay otros movimientos musicales?

—Era justamente lo que iba a decir. Un movimiento es el de la "Nueva Trova Cubana" con Silvio Rodríguez y Pablo Milanés, quienes cantan canciones de temas políticos, sociales y sentimentales. El otro movimiento importante es la "Nueva Canción" que nació en Chile en la década de los sesenta. Este tipo de música se conoció en el resto del mundo cuando Simon y Garfunkel incluyeron en un álbum "El cóndor pasa", una canción del conjunto Los Incas, quienes pertenecen a este movimiento. Sirven de inspiración para los cantantes de hoy.

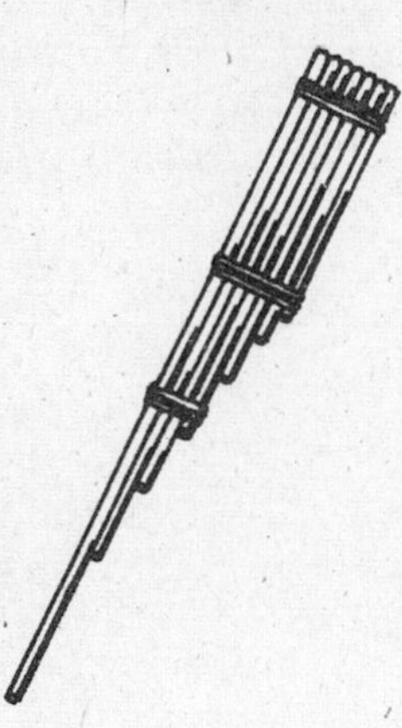

—Pero, ¿qué es la Nueva Canción?

—Es un estilo de música que tiene como elementos esenciales el uso de los ritmos e instrumentos tradicionales de los indígenas de los Andes. Las canciones son de protesta, o sea, de tema político, y critican la situación socioeconómica de los países hispanos. Pero, ahora este estilo de música se conoce en todo el mundo, y se puede oír a los músicos tocando en la calle o en los metros de ciudades de Copenhagan a Tokio.

[1]*Pablo Cuerda is a fictitious character.*

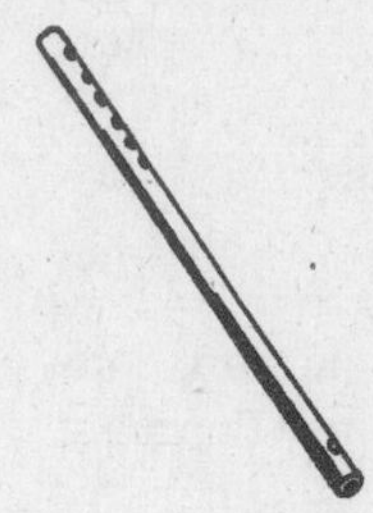

—**Y esto nos lleva a mi última pregunta. ¿Qué escucha la gente joven hoy día?**

—La gente joven escucha de todo: la Nueva Canción, rock nacional y extranjero, la Nueva Trova, rap, pop, rumba, guaracha, bachata, reggaetón y también cumbia, salsa y merengue, y los bailan muchísimo. Permíteme ahora tocarte una canción de Juan Luis Guerra, un innovador de la música hispanoamericana.

Y así terminó nuestra entrevista: con un ritmo y una melodía maravillosos.

Actividad 26 **Completa las ideas.** Después de leer la entrevista, escribe una o dos oraciones sobre cada una de las siguientes ideas relacionadas con el texto.

1. la guitarra ______________________________

   ____
2. los esclavos africanos ______________________________

   ____
3. la salsa ______________________________

   ____
4. "El cóndor pasa" ______________________________

   ____
5. La Nueva Trova ______________________________

   ____
6. La Nueva Canción ______________________________

   ____

Lab Manual

Nombre ______________________ Sección ______________ Fecha ____________

Capítulo preliminar

¡Bienvenidos!

Tips for Using the Lab Audio Program

1. Listen to and do the pronunciation section when you begin to study each chapter.
2. Do the rest of the lab activities after studying the grammar explanation in the second half of each chapter.
3. Read the directions and the items in each activity in your Lab Manual before listening to the audio.
4. You are not expected to understand every word you hear on the audio. All you need to be able to do is to comprehend enough information to complete the activities in the Lab Manual.
5. Listen to the audio as many times as may be needed. At first you may feel that the speakers speak too quickly; however, with practice you will find that it becomes easier as you become more comfortable listening to Spanish.

Mejora tu pronunciación

Stressing Words

You have already seen Spanish stress patterns in the text. Remember that a word that ends in *n, s,* or a vowel is stressed on the next-to-last syllable; for example, **re*pi*tan, Hon*du*ras, a*mi*go.** A word that ends in a consonant other than *n* or *s* is stressed on the last syllable; as in the words **espa*ñol,* fa*vor,* Ma*drid*.** Any exception to these two rules is indicated by a written accent mark on the stressed vowel, as in **An*drés,* Pe*rú,* *án*gel.**

Placing correct stress on words helps you to be better understood. For example, the word **a*mi*go** has its natural stress on the next-to-last syllable. Listen again: ***a*migo,** not ***a*migo,** nor **ami*go*; a*mi*go.** Try to keep stress in mind when learning new words.

Actividad 1 Escucha y subraya.

A. Listen to the following names of Hispanic countries and cities and underline the stressed syllables. You will hear each name twice.

1. Pa-na-ma
2. Bo-go-ta
3. Cu-ba
4. Ve-ne-zue-la
5. Me-xi-co
6. Ma-drid
7. Te-gu-ci-gal-pa
8. A-sun-cion

Continued on next page →

B. Pause the recording and decide which of the words from part A need written accents. Write the missing accents over the appropriate vowels.

Actividad 2 Los acentos.

A. Listen to the following words related to an office and underline the stressed syllables. You will hear each word twice.

1. o-fi-ci-na
2. di-rec-tor
3. pa-pel
4. dis-cu-sion
5. te-le-fo-no
6. bo-li-gra-fo
7. se-cre-ta-rio
8. ins-truc-cio-nes

B. Pause the recording and decide which of the words from part A need written accents. Write the missing accents over the appropriate vowels.

Mejora tu comprensión

Actividad 3 La fiesta. You will hear three introductions at a party. Indicate whether each one is formal or informal.

	Formal	Informal
1.	☐	☐
2.	☐	☐
3.	☐	☐

Nombre ______________________ Sección ______________ Fecha ____________

Actividad 4 **¿De dónde eres?** You will hear three conversations. Don't worry if you can't understand every word. Just concentrate on discovering where the people in the pictures are from. Write this information on the lines provided.

1. ______________ 2. ______________ 3. ______________

Actividad 5 **¡Hola! ¡Adiós!** You will hear three conversations. Don't worry if you can't understand every word. Just concentrate on discovering whether the people are greeting each other or saying good-by.

	Saludo (*greeting*)	Despedida (*saying good-by*)
1.	❐	❐
2.	❐	❐
3.	❐	❐

Actividad 6 **La entrevista.** A man is interviewing a woman for a job. You will only hear what the man is saying. As you listen, number the response that the woman should logically make to each of the interviewer's statements and questions. Before listening to the interview, pause the recording, and look at the woman's possible responses. You may have to listen to the interview more than once.

________ Gracias.

________ Soy de Caracas.

________ Claudia Menéndez.

________ ¡Muy bien!

Actividad 7 **Las capitales.** You will hear a series of questions on the capitals of various countries. Select the correct answers. Before listening to each question, pause the recording and read the three possible responses.

1.	Washington, D.C.	San Salvador	Lima
2.	México	Guatemala	Madrid
3.	Ottawa	Washington, D.C.	Buenos Aires
4.	Lima	Bogotá	Tegucigalpa
5.	Caracas	Santiago	Managua

Actividad 8 **Las órdenes.** You will hear a teacher give several commands. Number the picture that corresponds to each command. If necessary, pause the recording after each item.

____

____

____

____

Actividad 9 **Las siglas.** Listen and write the following acronyms.

1. ______________________
2. ______________________
3. ______________________
4. ______________________
5. ______________________
6. ______________________

Actividad 10 **¿Cómo se escribe?** You will hear two conversations. Concentrate on listening to the names that are spelled out within the conversations and write them down.

1. ______________________
2. ______________________

Capítulo 1 ¿Quién es?

Mejora tu pronunciación

Vowels

In Spanish, there are only five basic vowel sounds: **a, e, i, o, u.** These correspond to the five vowels of the alphabet. In contrast, English has long and short vowels; for example, the long *i* in *pie* and the short *i* in *pit.* In addition, English has the short sound, schwa, which is used to pronounce many unstressed vowels. For example, the first and last *a* in the word *banana* are unstressed and are therefore pronounced [ə]. Listen: *banana.* In Spanish, there is no similar sound because vowels are usually pronounced the same way whether they are stressed or not. Listen: **banana.**

Actividad 1 Escucha la diferencia. Listen to the contrast in vowel sounds between English and Spanish.

	Inglés	Español
1.	map	mapa
2.	net	neto
3.	beam	viga
4.	tone	tono
5.	taboo	tabú

Actividad 2 Escucha y repite. Listen and repeat the following names, paying special attention to the pronunciation of the vowel sounds.

1. Ana Lara
2. Pepe Méndez
3. Mimí Pinti
4. Toto Soto
5. Lulú Mumú

Actividad 3 **Repite las oraciones.** Listen and repeat the following sentences from the textbook conversations. Pay attention to the pronunciation of the vowel sounds.

1. ¿Cómo se llama Ud.?
2. Buenos días.
3. ¿Cómo se escribe?
4. ¿Quién es ella?
5. Juan Carlos es de Perú.
6. Las dos Coca-Colas.

Mejora tu comprensión

Actividad 4 **Guatemala.** You will hear a series of numbers. Draw a line to connect these numbers in the order in which you hear them. When you finish, you will have a map of Guatemala.

1	2	3	4	5	6	7	8	9	10
11	12	13	14	15	16	17	18	19	20
21	22	23	24	25	26	27	28	29	30
31	32	33	34	35	36	37	38	39	40
41	42	43	44	45	46	47	48	49	50
51	52	53	54	55	56	57	58	59	60
61	62	63	64	65	66	67	68	69	70
71	72	73	74	75	76	77	78	79	80
81	82	83	84	85	86	87	88	89	90
91	92	93	94	95	96	97	98	99	100

Actividad 5 **Los números de teléfono.** You will hear a telephone conversation and two recorded messages. Don't worry if you can't understand every word. Just concentrate on writing down the telephone number that is given in each case.

1. ____________________ 2. ____________________ 3. ____________________

Nombre ______________________ Sección ______________ Fecha ______________

Actividad 6 **¿Él o ella?** Listen to the following three conversations and select the person who is being talked about in each case. Don't worry if you can't understand every word. Just concentrate on discovering to whom each discussion refers.

1. ☐ ☐ 2. ☐ ☐ 3. ☐ ☐

Actividad 7 **En el tren.** Carlos is talking to a woman with a child on the train. Listen to the four questions that he asks. For each of the four questions, number the appropriate response one to four. Note that there is one extra response below that will not be used. Before you begin the activity, pause the recording and read the possible responses.

_______ Dos años. _______ De Tegucigalpa.

_______ Andrea. _______ Ella se llama Deborah.

_______ Son de México.

Actividad 8 **La conversación.**

A. You will hear a series of sentences. Write each sentence or pairs of sentences you hear in the first column below. Be sure to use correct capitalization and punctuation. You will hear each sentence or pair of sentences twice.

A. ______________________	______
B. ______________________	______
C. ______________________	______
D. ______________________	______
E. ______________________	______
F. ______________________	______
G. ______________________	______
H. ______________________	______

Continued on next page →

B. Now stop the recording and put the sentences you have written in the correct order to form a logical conversation. Number each sentence in the blank in the right-hand column above.

Actividad 9 **En el hotel.** You will hear a conversation between a hotel receptionist and a guest who is registering. Fill out the computer screen with the information about the guest. Don't worry if you can't understand every word. Just concentrate on listening for the information needed. You may have to listen to the conversation more than once. Remember to look at the computer screen before you begin the activity.

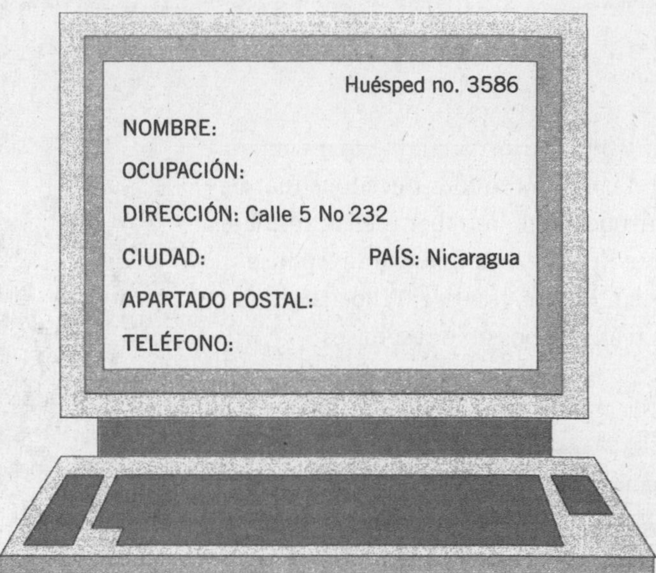

Huésped no. 3586
NOMBRE:
OCUPACIÓN:
DIRECCIÓN: Calle 5 No 232
CIUDAD:
PAÍS: Nicaragua
APARTADO POSTAL:
TELÉFONO:

Actividad 10 **Los participantes.** Mr. Torres and his assistant are going over the participants they have chosen for a TV game show. Listen to their conversation and fill out the chart with information on the participants. Don't worry if you can't understand every word. Just concentrate on listening for the information needed to complete the chart. You may have to listen to the conversation more than once.

Participantes	Nacionalidad	Ocupación	Edad
Francisco	*chileno*		
Laura		*abogada*	
Gonzalo			*30*
Andrea	*mexicana*		

Conversación: En el Colegio Mayor Hispanoamericano
Conversación: En la cafetería del colegio mayor

Nombre ______________________ Sección ______________ Fecha ____________

Capítulo 2 ¿Te gusta?

Mejora tu pronunciación

The consonant *d*

The consonant **d** is pronounced two different ways in Spanish. When **d** appears at the beginning of a word or after *n* or *l*, it is pronounced by pressing the tongue against the back of the teeth; for example, **depósito.** When **d** appears after a vowel, after a consonant other than *n* or *l*, or at the end of a word, it is pronounced like the *th* in the English word *they*; for example, **médico.**

Actividad 1 **Escucha y repite.** Listen and repeat the names of the following occupations, paying attention to the pronunciation of the letter **d.**

1. **d**irector
2. **d**eportista
3. ven**d**e**d**or
4. mé**d**ico
5. estu**d**iante
6. aboga**d**a

Spanish *p, t,* and *[k]*

In Spanish, **p, t,** and **[k]** (**[k]** represents a sound) are unaspirated. This means that no puff of air occurs when they are pronounced. Listen to the difference: *Paul,* **Pablo.**

Actividad 2 **Escucha y repite.** Listen and repeat the names of the following objects often found around the house. Pay attention to the pronunciation of **p, t,** and **[k].**

1. **p**eriódi**c**o
2. **t**eléfono
3. **c**om**p**u**t**adora
4. **t**elevisor
5. **c**ámara
6. dis**c**o **c**om**p**a**ct**o

Actividad 3 **Las cosas de Marisel.** Listen and repeat the following conversation between Teresa and Marisel. Pay attention to the pronunciation of **p, t,** and **[k].**

TERESA ¿**T**ienes **c**afé?
MARISEL ¡**C**laro **qu**e sí!
TERESA ¡Ah! **T**ienes **c**om**p**u**t**adora.
MARISEL Sí, es una Ma**c**in**t**osh. Me gus**t**a la Ma**c**in**t**osh.
TERESA ¿De veras? A mí no me gus**t**a la Ma**c**.

Mejora tu comprensión

Actividad 4 **La perfumería.** You will hear a conversation in a drugstore between a customer and a salesclerk. Select only the products that the customer buys and indicate whether she buys one or more than one of each item. Don't worry if you can't understand every word. Just concentrate on the customer's purchases. Before you listen to the conversation, read the list of products.

	Uno/a	Más de uno/a (*more than one*)
1. aspirina	☐	☐
2. crema de afeitar	☐	☐
3. champú	☐	☐
4. cepillo de dientes	☐	☐
5. desodorante	☐	☐
6. jabón	☐	☐
7. pasta de dientes	☐	☐
8. peine	☐	☐
9. perfume	☐	☐

Actividad 5 **El baño de las chicas.** Alelí, Teresa's young cousin, is visiting her at the dorm and she is now in the bathroom asking Teresa a lot of questions. As you hear the conversation, indicate in the drawing which of the items mentioned belong to whom.

Nombre ______________________ Sección ______________ Fecha ____________

Actividad 6 **¿Hombre o mujer?** Listen to the following remarks and select the person or persons being described in each situation.

1. ______ ______ 2. ______ ______

3. ______ ______ 4. ______ ______

Actividad 7 **El mensaje telefónico.** Ms. Rodríguez calls home and leaves a message on the answering machine for her children, Esteban and Carina. Ms. Rodríguez reminds them to do four things. Select each item that she reminds them about. Before you listen to the message, pause the recording and read the list of reminders. Notice there are five items in the list and she only mentions four. Don't worry if you can't understand every word. Just concentrate on which reminders are for Esteban and which ones are for Carina.

	Esteban	Carina
1. comprar hamburguesas	☐	☐
2. llamar a Carlos	☐	☐
3. estudiar matemáticas	☐	☐
4. mirar un DVD	☐	☐
5. no ir al dentista	☐	☐

Actividad 8 **El regalo de cumpleaños.**

A. You will hear a phone conversation between Álvaro and his mother, who would like to know what she can buy him for his birthday. Select the things that Álvaro says he already has. Don't worry if you can't understand every word. Just concentrate on what Álvaro doesn't need. Before you listen to the conversation, read the list of items.

Álvaro tiene...

☐ escritorio ☐ lámpara ☐ reloj ☐ silla ☐ toallas

B. Now write what Álvaro's mother is going to give him for his birthday. You may need to listen to the conversation again.

El regalo es ______________________________.

Actividad 9 **La agenda de Diana.**

A. Pause the recording and write in Spanish two things you are going to do this weekend.

1. ____

2. ____

B. Now complete Diana's calendar while you listen to Diana and Claudia talking on the phone about their weekend plans. Don't worry if you can't understand every word. Just concentrate on Diana's plans. You may have to listen to the conversation more than once.

DÍA	ACTIVIDADES
viernes	3:00 P.M. –examen de literatura
sábado	
domingo	

Actividad 10 **La conexión amorosa.** Mónica has gone to a dating service and has made a tape describing her likes and dislikes. Listen to the recording and then choose a suitable man for her from the two shown. Don't worry if you can't understand every word. Just concentrate on Mónica's preferences. You may use the following space to take notes. Before you listen to the description, read the information on the two men.

A Mónica le gusta:

NOMBRE: Óscar Varone
OCUPACIÓN: profesor de historia
EDAD: 32
GUSTOS: música salsa, escribir

NOMBRE: Lucas González
OCUPACIÓN: médico
EDAD: 30
GUSTOS: música clásica, salsa, esquiar

El hombre perfecto para Mónica es ______________________________ .
(nombre)

Conversación: ¡Me gusta mucho!
Conversación: Planes para una fiesta de bienvenida

Nombre ______________________ Sección ______________ Fecha ____________

Capítulo 3 Un día típico

Mejora tu pronunciación

The consonants *r* and *rr*

The consonant **r** in Spanish has two different pronunciations: the flap, as in **caro,** similar to the double *t* sound in *butter* and *petty,* and the trill sound, as in **carro.** The **r** is pronounced with the trill only at the beginning of a word or after *l* or *n,* as in **reservado, sonrisa** (*smile*). The **rr** is always pronounced with the trill, as in **aburrido.**

Actividad 1 Escucha y repite. Listen and repeat the following descriptive words. Pay attention to the pronunciation of the consonants **r** and **rr.**

1. enfermo
2. rubio
3. moreno
4. gordo
5. aburrido
6. enamorado
7. preocupado
8. borracho

Actividad 2 Escucha y marca la diferencia. Circle the word you hear pronounced in each of the following word pairs. Before you begin, look over the pictures and word pairs.

1. caro carro
2. coro corro

3. ahora ahorra
4. cero cerro

Actividad 3 **Teresa.** Listen and repeat the following sentences about Teresa. Pay attention to the pronunciation of the consonants **r** and **rr.**

1. Estudia turismo.
2. Trabaja en una agencia de viajes.
3. Su papá es un actor famoso de Puerto Rico.
4. ¿Pero ella es puertorriqueña?

Mejora tu comprensión

Actividad 4 **¿Dónde?** You will hear four remarks. Match the letter of each remark with the place where it is most likely to be heard. Before you listen to the remarks, review the list of places. Notice that there are extra place names.

1. _______ farmacia
2. _______ biblioteca
3. _______ teatro
4. _______ supermercado
5. _______ agencia de viajes
6. _______ librería

Actividad 5 **Mi niña es...** A man has lost his daughter in a department store and is describing her to the store detective. Listen to his description and place a check mark below the drawing of the child he is looking for. Don't worry if you can't understand every word. Just concentrate on the father's description of the child. Before you listen to the conversation, look at the drawings.

1. ☐

2. ☐

3. ☐

Nombre ______________________________ Sección ________________ Fecha ____________

Actividad 6 **Su hijo está...** Use the words in the list to complete the chart about Pablo as you hear a conversation between his teacher and his mother. Fill in **en general** to describe the way Pablo usually is. Fill in **esta semana** to indicate how he has been behaving this week.

aburrido	**antipático**	**bueno**
cansado	**inteligente**	**simpático**

Pablo Hernández
En general, él es ____
____.
Pero, esta semana él está _______________________________________
____.

Actividad 7 **La conversación telefónica.** Teresa is talking with her father long-distance. You will hear her father's portion of the conversation only. After you hear each of the father's questions, complete Teresa's partial replies.

1. ____________ ____________________ Claudia.
2. ____________________ economía.
3. ____________ ____________ la Universidad Complutense.
4. ____________ de Colombia.
5. ____________, pero ahora ____________________ en Quito.
6. ____________ es comerciante.
7. ____________ ama de casa.
8. ____________________, gracias.
9. ____________, ____________________ mucho.
10. ____________________ en la agencia de viajes del tío Alejandro.
11. ____________________ muy ocupado.

Actividad 8 **Intercambio estudiantil.** Marcos contacts a student-exchange program in order to have a foreign student stay with him. Complete the following form as you hear his conversation with the program's secretary. Don't worry if you can't understand every word. Just concentrate on filling out the form. Before you listen to the conversation, read the form.

C.A.D.I.E.: CONSEJO ARGENTINO DE INTERCAMBIO ESTUDIANTIL		
Nombre del interesado: *Marcos Alarcón*		
Teléfono:		
Móvil:	Edad:	Ocupación:
Gustos: *leer ciencia ficción*		
Preferencia de nacionalidad:		

Actividad 9 **Las descripciones.**

A. Choose three adjectives from the list of personality characteristics that best describe each of the people shown. Pause the recording while you make your selection.

artístico/a	intelectual	inteligente
optimista	paciente	pesimista
serio/a	simpático/a	tímido/a

Tu opinión

1. ______________________
____
____

Tu opinión

2. ______________________
____
____

B. Now listen as these two people describe themselves, and enter these adjectives in the blanks provided. You may have to listen to the descriptions more than once.

Su descripción

1. ______________________
____
____

Su descripción

2. ______________________
____
____

Nombre ______________________ Sección ______________ Fecha ____________

Actividad 10 **El detective Alonso.** Detective Alonso is speaking into his tape recorder while following a woman. Number the drawings in the upper left corner according to the order in which he says the events take place. Don't worry if you can't understand every word. Just concentrate on the sequence of events.

Conversación: Una llamada de larga distancia
Conversación: Hay familias... y... FAMILIAS

Nombre ______________________ Sección ______________ Fecha ____________

Capítulo 4 ¿Tarde o temprano?

Mejora tu pronunciación

The consonant *ñ*

The pronunciation of the consonant **ñ** is similar to the *ny* in the English word *canyon.*

Actividad 1 **Escucha y repite.** Listen and repeat the following words, paying attention to the pronunciation of the consonants **n** and **ñ**.

1. cana caña
2. una uña
3. mono moño
4. sonar soñar

Actividad 2 **Escucha y repite.** Listen and repeat the following sentences. Pay special attention to the pronunciation of the consonants **n** and **ñ**.

1. Subo **una** mo**n**ta**ñ**a.
2. Trabajo co**n** **niñ**os que **n**o tie**n**e**n** padres.
3. Tú co**n**oces al se**ñ**or de Rodrigo, ¿**n**o?
4. ¿Cuá**n**do es tu cumplea**ñ**os?

Mejora tu comprensión

Actividad 3 **Los sonidos de la mañana.** Listen to the following sounds and write what Paco is doing this morning.

1. ______________________________
2. ______________________________
3. ______________________________
4. ______________________________

Actividad 4 **El tiempo este fin de semana.**

A. As you hear this weekend's weather forecast for Argentina, draw the corresponding weather symbols on the map under the names of the places mentioned. Remember to read the place names on the map and look at the symbols before you listen to the forecast.

B. Now replay the activity and listen to the forecast again, this time adding the temperatures in Celsius under the names of the places mentioned.

Nombre ______________________ Sección ______________ Fecha ____________

Actividad 5 **La identificación del ladrón.** As you hear a woman describing a thief to a police artist, complete the artist's sketch. You may have to replay the activity and listen to the description more than once.

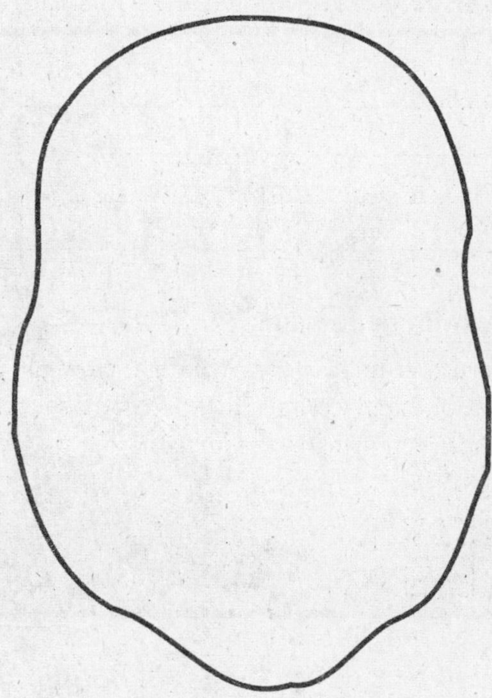

Actividad 6 **Celebraciones hispanas.**

A. A woman will describe some important holidays around the Hispanic world. As you listen to the description of each holiday, write the date on which it is celebrated.

	Fecha
1. Día de los Muertos	______________________
2. Día de los Santos Inocentes	______________________
3. Día Internacional del Amigo	______________________
4. Día de Reyes	______________________

B. Now listen again and match the holiday with the activity people usually do on that day. Write the number of the holiday from the preceding list.

a. __________ las personas reciben emails de otras personas

b. __________ las personas hacen bromas (*pranks*)

c. __________ las personas hacen un altar en casa

d. __________ los niños reciben juguetes (*toys*)

Actividad 7 ¿Conoces a ese chico?

A. Miriam and Julio are discussing some guests at a party. As you listen to their conversation, write the guests' names in the drawing. Use arrows to indicate which name goes with which person.

B. Now listen to the conversation again, and next to each name write who the person knows or what the person knows how to do using **conocer** or **saber**.

Actividad 8 La entrevista.

Lola Drones, a newspaper reporter, is interviewing a famous actor about his weekend habits. Cross out those activities listed in Lola's notebook that the actor does *not* do on weekends. Remember to read the list of possible activities before you listen to the interview.

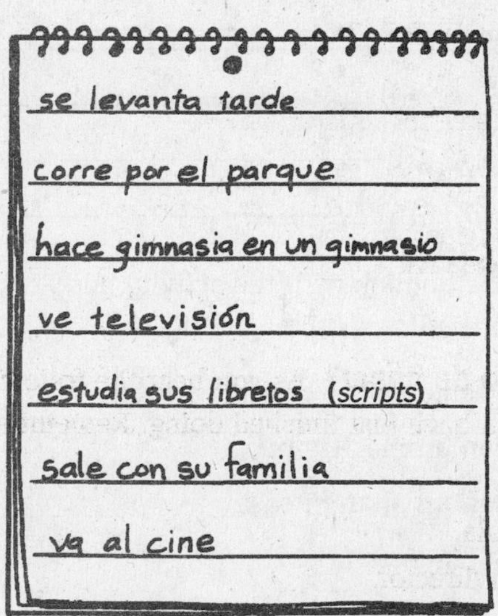

se levanta tarde
corre por el parque
hace gimnasia en un gimnasio
ve televisión
estudia sus libretos (scripts)
sale con su familia
va al cine

Conversación: Noticias de una amiga
Conversación: El mensaje telefónico

Nombre ______________________ Sección ______________ Fecha __________

Capítulo 5

Los planes y las compras

Mejora tu pronunciación

The consonants *ll* and *y*

The consonants **ll** and **y** are usually pronounced like the *y* in the English word *yellow.* When the **y** appears at the end of a word, or alone, it is pronounced like the vowel **i** in Spanish.

Actividad 1 **Escucha y repite.** Listen and repeat the following verse. Pay special attention to the pronunciation of the **ll** and the **y**.

Hay una toa**ll**a
en la pla**y**a amari**ll**a.

Ho**y** no **ll**ueve.
E**ll**a no tiene si**ll**a.

Actividad 2 **Escucha y repite.** Listen and repeat the following sentences. Pay special attention to the pronunciation of the **ll** and the **y**.

1. **Y** por favor, otra cerveza.
2. ¿Tiene por casualidad un periódico de ho**y**?
3. Se come mu**y** bien a**ll**í.
4. **Y** entonces, como es su cumpleaños, e**ll**a invita.

Mejora tu comprensión

Actividad 3 **¿Qué acaban de hacer?** As you hear the following short conversations, select what the people in each situation have just finished doing. Remember to read the list of possible activities before you begin.

1. a. Acaban de ver una película.
   b. Acaban de hablar con un director.
2. a. Acaban de beber un café.
   b. Acaban de comer.
3. a. Acaban de ducharse.
   b. Acaban de jugar un partido de fútbol.

Actividad 4 **El cine.** You will hear a recorded message and a conversation, both about movie schedules. As you listen, complete the information on the cards. Don't worry if you can't understand every word. Just concentrate on filling out the cards. Remember to look at the cards before beginning.

GRAN REX

La historia oficial

Horario: ____________, ____________, ____________, 10:00

Precio: $____________ $____________ matinée.

SPLENDID

La mujer cucaracha

Horario: ____________, 8:00, ____________

Precio: $____________ $____________ matinée.

Actividad 5 **Las citas del Dr. Malapata.** As you hear Dr. Malapata's receptionist making appointments for two patients, complete the corresponding scheduling cards.

DR. MALAPATA

Paciente:

Fecha: Hora:

Fecha de hoy:

DR. MALAPATA

Paciente:

Fecha: Hora:

Fecha de hoy:

Nombre ______________________ Sección ______________ Fecha ____________

Actividad 6 **Las sensaciones.** Listen to the conversation between Alberto and Dora, and select the different sensations or feelings they have. Read the list of sensations and feelings before you listen to the conversation. Note that there are extra sentences.

	Alberto	Dora
1. Tiene calor.	❒	❒
2. Tiene frío.	❒	❒
3. Tiene hambre.	❒	❒
4. Tiene miedo.	❒	❒
5. Tiene sed.	❒	❒
6. Tiene sueño.	❒	❒
7. Tiene vergüenza.	❒	❒

Actividad 7 **Ofertas increíbles.** Listen to the following radio ad about a department store and select the articles of clothing that are mentioned. Remember to read the list of items before you listen to the ad.

______ blusas de cuadros

______ blusas de rayas

______ camisas de manga corta

______ camisas de manga larga

______ chaquetas de cuero

______ cinturones de plástico

______ faldas de seda

______ trajes de baño de algodón

______ zapatos de diferentes colores

Actividad 8 **La fiesta.**

A. Look at the drawing of a party and write four sentences in Spanish describing what some of the guests are doing. Pause the recording while you write.

Pablo

____

Fabiana

____

Lucía

____

Mariana

____

1. ____

2. ____

3. ____

4. ____

Continued on next page →

B. Miriam and Julio are discussing some of the guests at the party. As you listen to their conversation, write the guests' names in the drawing. Use arrows to indicate which name goes with which person. Don't worry if you can't understand every word. Just concentrate on who's who.

C. Now listen to the conversation again and write the occupations of the four guests below their names.

Actividad 9 Los fines de semana.

A. Write three sentences in Spanish describing things you usually do on weekends. Pause the recording while you write.

1. ____
2. ____
3. ____

B. Pedro is on the phone talking to his father about what he and his roommate Mario do on weekends. Listen to their conversation and select Pedro's activities versus Mario's. Remember to read the list of activities before you listen to the conversation.

	Pedro	Mario
1. Se acuesta temprano.	❐	❐
2. Se acuesta tarde.	❐	❐
3. Sale con sus amigos.	❐	❐
4. Se despierta temprano.	❐	❐
5. Se despierta tarde.	❐	❐
6. Duerme 10 horas.	❐	❐
7. Duerme 14 horas.	❐	❐
8. Juega al fútbol.	❐	❐
9. Almuerza con sus amigos.	❐	❐
10. Pide una pizza.	❐	❐
11. Juega al tenis.	❐	❐

Conversación: ¿Qué hacemos esta noche?
Conversación: De compras en San Juan

Nombre ______________________ Sección ______________ Fecha ____________

Mejora tu pronunciación

The sound [*g*]

The sound represented by the letter *g* before *a, o,* and *u* is pronounced a little softer than the English *g* in the word *guy:* **gustar, regalo, tengo.** Because the combinations **ge** and **gi** are pronounced **[he]** and **[hi]**, a *u* is added after the *g* to retain the **[g]** sound: **guitarra, guerra.**

Actividad 1 **Escucha y repite.** Listen and repeat the following phrases, paying special attention to the pronunciation of the letter **g**.

1. mi ami**g**a
2. te **g**ustó
3. es ele**g**ante
4. sabes al**g**o
5. no ten**g**o
6. no pa**gu**é

Actividad 2 **¡Qué guapo!** Listen and repeat the following conversation between Claudio and Marisa. Pay special attention to the pronunciation of the letter **g**.

MARISA Me **gu**stan mucho.
CLAUDIO ¿Mis bi**g**otes?
MARISA Sí, estás **gu**apo pero cansado, ¿no?
CLAUDIO Es que ju**gu**é al tenis.
MARISA ¿Con **G**ómez?
CLAUDIO No, con López, el **gu**ía de turismo.

The sound [*k*]

The **[k]** sound in Spanish is unaspirated, as in the words **casa, claro, quitar,** and **kilo.** Hear the contrast between the *[k]* sound in English where a puff of air comes out as one pronounces the letter, and the **[k]** sound in Spanish where there is no puff of air: *case,* **caso;** *kilo,* **kilo;** *cape,* **capa.** The **[k]** sound in Spanish is spelled *c* before *a, o,* and *u; qu* before *e* and *i;* and *k* in a few words of foreign origin such as **kiwi, karate, kilómetro.** Remember that the *u* is not pronounced in *que* or *qui,* as in the words **qué** and **quitar.**

Actividad 3 **El saco.** Listen and repeat the following conversation between a salesclerk and a customer. Pay attention to the [**k**] sound.

CLIENTE ¿**Cu**ánto **cu**esta ese sa**co**?

VENDEDORA ¿A**que**l?

CLIENTE Sí, el de **cu**ero negro.

VENDEDORA ¿No **qui**ere el sa**co** azul?

CLIENTE No. Bus**co** uno negro.

Mejora tu comprensión

Actividad 4 **El gran almacén.** You are in Falabella, a department store in Chile, and you hear about the sales of the day over the loudspeaker system. As you listen, write the correct price above each of the items shown. Remember that Spanish uses periods where English uses commas and vice versa: **3.500 pesos.**

Nombre ______________________ Sección ________________ Fecha ____________

Actividad 5 Los premios.

A. You will listen to a radio ad for a photo contest that mentions the prizes (**premios**) that will be awarded and how much each is worth. Before you listen to the ad, stop the recording and write down under **tu opinión** how much you think each item is worth in dollars.

	tu opinión	**el anuncio (*ad*)**
Mercedes-Benz	$ ____________	$ ____________
viaje para dos por una semana a Las Vegas	$ ____________	$ ____________
reproductor de DVD	$ ____________	$ ____________
cámara digital	$ ____________	$ ____________
chaqueta de cuero	$ ____________	$ ____________

B. Now listen to the ad and write down how much each prize is worth in Mexican pesos in the second column.

Actividad 6 La habitación de Vicente.

Vicente is angry because Juan Carlos, his roommate, is very messy. As you listen to Vicente describing the mess to Álvaro, write the names of the following objects in the drawing of the room, according to where Juan Carlos leaves them.

medias **teléfono** **libros** **periódico**

Actividad 7 **¿Presente o pasado?** As you listen to each of the following remarks, select whether the speaker is talking about the present or the past.

	Presente	Pasado
1.	❐	❐
2.	❐	❐
3.	❐	❐
4.	❐	❐

Actividad 8 **El fin de semana pasado.**

A. Write in Spanish three things you did last weekend. Pause the recording while you write.

1. ______________________________
2. ______________________________
3. ______________________________

B. Now listen to Raúl and Alicia talking in the office about what they did last weekend. Write **R** next to the things that Raúl did, and **A** next to the things that Alicia did. Remember to look at the list of activities before you listen to the conversation.

1. ________ Fue a una fiesta.
2. ________ Trabajó.
3. ________ Comió en su casa.
4. ________ Se acostó temprano.
5. ________ Fue al cine.
6. ________ Tomó café.
7. ________ Habló con una amiga.
8. ________ Se acostó tarde.
9. ________ Jugó al tenis.
10. ________ Miró TV.

Actividad 9 **La familia de Álvaro.** This is an incomplete tree of Álvaro's family. As you listen to the conversation between Álvaro and Clara, complete the tree with the initials of the names listed. Don't be concerned if you don't understand every word. Just concentrate on completing the family tree. You may have to listen to the conversation more than once.

Juan José **Flavia** **Héctor** **Tomás**

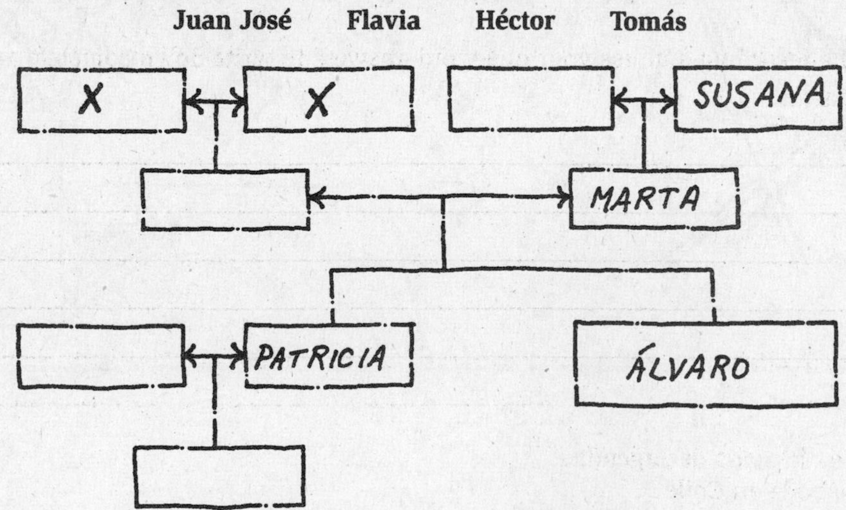

Nombre ____________________ Sección ______________ Fecha ____________

Actividad 10 **Una cena familiar.** Tonight there is a family dinner at Álvaro's and his mother is planning the seating arrangements. Listen to Álvaro's mother, Marta, as she explains her plan to Álvaro. Write the name of each family member on the card in front of his/her place setting. You may have to refer to **Actividad 9** for the names of some of Álvaro's relatives.

Actividad 11 **El matrimonio de Nando y Olga.**

A. Nando and Olga have already gotten married, and now Hernán, Nando's father, gets a phone call. Read the questions; then listen to the phone call and jot one-word answers next to each question. You may have to listen to the conversation more than once.

1. ¿Quién llamó al padre de Nando por teléfono? ____________
2. ¿A quién le hizo un vestido la Sra. Montedio? ____________
3. ¿Qué le alquiló la mamá de Nando a su hijo? ____________
4. ¿Quién les regaló una cámara de video a los novios? ____________
5. ¿Quiénes les regalaron un viaje? ____________
6. ¿A quiénes llamaron los novios desde la República Dominicana? ____________

B. Now pause the recording and use your one-word answers to write down complete answers to the questions from part A.

1. ____________
2. ____________
3. ____________
4. ____________
5. ____________
6. ____________

Conversación: Una llamada de Argentina
Conversación: La boda en Chile

Nombre ______________________ Sección ______________ Fecha __________

Capítulo 7

Los viajes

Mejora tu pronunciación

The consonants *b* and *v*

In Spanish, there is generally no difference between the pronunciation of the consonants **b** and **v.** When they occur at the beginning of a sentence, after a pause, or after *m* or *n,* they are pronounced like the *b* in the English word *bay;* for example, **bolso, vuelo, ambos, envío.** In all other cases, they are pronounced by not quite closing the lips, as in **cabeza** and **nuevo.**

Actividad 1 **Escucha y repite.** Listen and repeat the following travel-related words, paying special attention to the pronunciation of the initial **b** and **v.**

1. **b**anco
2. **v**estido
3. **v**uelo
4. **b**olso
5. **v**uelta
6. **b**otones

Actividad 2 **Escucha y repite.** Listen and repeat the following weather expressions. Note the pronunciation of **b** and **v** when they occur within a phrase.

1. Está nu**b**lado.
2. Hace **b**uen tiempo.
3. ¿Cuánto **v**iento hace?
4. Llue**v**e mucho.
5. Está a dos grados **b**ajo cero.

Actividad 3 **En el aeropuerto.** Listen and repeat the following sentences. Pay special attention to the pronunciation of **b** and **v.**

1. **B**uen **v**iaje.
2. ¿Y su hijo **v**iaja solo o con Ud.?
3. Las lle**v**as en la mano.
4. ¿Dónde pongo las **b**otellas de ron?
5. **V**amos a hacer escala en Miami.
6. Pero no lo **v**a a **b**e**b**er él.
7. **V**oy a cam**b**iar mi pasaje.

Mejora tu comprensión

Actividad 4 **¿Qué es?** As you hear each of the following short conversations in a department store, select the object that the people are discussing.

1. ☐ una blusa ☐ un saco
2. ☐ unos pantalones ☐ un sombrero
3. ☐ unas camas ☐ unos DVDs

Actividad 5 **Un mensaje para Teresa.** Vicente calls Teresa at work, but she is not there. Instead, he talks with Alejandro, Teresa's uncle. As you listen to their conversation, write the message that Vicente leaves.

MENSAJE TELEFÓNICO

Para: *Teresa*

Llamó: ______

Teléfono: ______

Mensaje: ______

Recibido por:	**Fecha:**	**Hora:**
tío Alejandro	*6 de septiembre*	

Actividad 6 **La operadora.** You will hear two telephone conversations. For each situation, select what happens.

1. ☐ tiene el número equivocado ☐ no comprende a la persona
2. ☐ quiere el indicativo del país ☐ quiere el prefijo de la ciudad

Actividad 7 **Las excusas.** Two of Perla's friends call her to apologize for not having come to her party last night. They also explain why some others didn't show up. As you listen, match each person with his or her excuse for not going to the party. Before you listen, stop the recording and read the excuses. Notice that there are extra excuses.

Invitados	**Excusas**
1. ______ Esteban	a. Tuvo que estudiar.
2. ______ Pilar	b. No le gusta salir cuando llueve.
3. ______ Andrés	c. Conoció a una persona en la calle.
4. ______ Viviana	d. Se durmió en el sofá.
	e. No pudo dejar a su hermano solo.
	f. Se acostó temprano.

Actividad 8 **Aeropuerto Internacional, buenos días.** You will hear three people calling the airport to ask about arriving flights. As you listen to the conversations, fill in the missing information on the arrival board.

LLEGADAS INTERNACIONALES				
Línea aérea	**Número de vuelo**	**Procedencia**	**Hora de llegada**	**Comentarios**
Iberia		Lima		a tiempo
TACA	357		12:15	
LACSA		NY/México		

Actividad 9 **Las noticias.** As you hear the news report, complete the following chart indicating who the people are and what happened in each case.

	Quién es	Qué ocurrió
1. María Salinas	________	____________________
2. Mario Valori	________	____________________
3. Pablo Bravo	________	____________________
4. Sara Méndez	________	____________________

Actividad 10 **¿Cuánto tiempo hace que...?** You will listen to a set of personal questions. Pause the recording after you listen to each question, and write a complete answer.

1. ____
2. ____
3. ____
4. ____

Actividad 11 **Mi primer trabajo.** As you listen to Mariano tell about his first job, fill in each of the blanks in his story with one or more words. Pause the recording and read the paragraph before you listen to Mariano.

______________________________ cuando empecé mi primer trabajo.
______________________________ cuando llegué a la oficina el primer día. Allí conocí a mis colegas. Todos eran muy simpáticos. Una persona estaba enferma, así que yo ______________________ todo el santo día. ______________________ de la mañana cuando terminé. Ése fue un día difícil pero feliz.

Actividad 12 **El horario de Nélida.** After you hear what Nélida did this evening, figure out when each event happened. You may want to listen more than once.

¿Qué hora era cuando pasaron estas cosas?

1. Nélida llegó a casa. ______________________________
2. Alguien la llamó. ______________________________
3. Entró en la bañera. ______________________________
4. Comenzó "Los Simpson". ______________________________
5. Se durmió. ______________________________

Conversación: ¿En un "banco" de Segovia?
Conversación: Un día normal en el aeropuerto

Nombre ______________________ Sección ______________ Fecha ____________

Capítulo 8 La comida y los deportes

Mejora tu pronunciación

Diphthongs

In Spanish, vowels are classified as weak (**i, u**) or strong (**a, e, o**). A diphthong is a combination of two weak vowels or a strong and a weak vowel in the same syllable. When a strong and a weak vowel are combined in the same syllable, the strong vowel takes a slightly greater stress; for example, **vuelvo.** When two weak vowels are combined, the second one takes a slightly greater stress, as in the word **ciudad.** Sometimes the weak vowel in a strong-weak combination takes a written accent, and the diphthong is therefore dissolved and two separate syllables are created. Listen to the contrast between the endings of these two words: **farmacia, policía.**

Actividad 1 **Escucha y repite.** Listen and repeat the following words.

1. las habich**ue**las
2. el ma**í**z
3. los cub**ie**rtos
4. la zanahor**ia**
5. la v**ai**nilla
6. c**ui**dar

Actividad 2 **Escucha y repite.** Listen and repeat the following sentences from the textbook conversation between Vicente and his parents.

1. S**ie**mpre los echo de menos.
2. B**ue**no, ahora vamos a ir a Sarchí.
3. Ten**ía** tres años c**ua**ndo subí a la carreta del ab**ue**lo.
4. No me s**ie**nto b**ie**n.
5. Q**uie**ren comprarle algo de artesan**ía** típica.

Actividad 3 **¿Diptongo o no?** Listen and mark whether the following words have a diphthong or not.

	Sí	No
1.	❐	❐
2.	❐	❐
3.	❐	❐
4.	❐	❐
5.	❐	❐
6.	❐	❐
7.	❐	❐

Mejora tu comprensión

Actividad 4 **¿Le molesta o le gusta?** As you listen to a series of statements, select the opinion of the speaker.

1. a. Las clases le parecieron fáciles.
   b. Las clases le parecieron difíciles.
2. a. Le encanta ir a la casa de sus padres.
   b. Le molesta ir a la casa de sus padres.
3. a. Le fascina la luz.
   b. Le molesta la luz.
4. a. A él le pareció interesante la película.
   b. A él le pareció aburrida la película.

Actividad 5 **Las compras.** Doña Emilia is going to send her son Ramón grocery shopping and is now figuring out what they need. As you listen to their conversation, select the items they have, those they need to buy, and those they are going to borrow from a neighbor.

	Tienen	Necesitan comprar	Van a pedir prestado (*borrow*)
1. aceite	❐	❐	❐
2. lechuga	❐	❐	❐
3. pan	❐	❐	❐
4. vino blanco	❐	❐	❐
5. pimienta	❐	❐	❐
6. vinagre	❐	❐	❐

Nombre ______________________ Sección ________________ Fecha ____________

Actividad 6 **En el restaurante.** A family is ordering in a restaurant. Listen to them place their order and select what each person wants.

Mesa No. 8			**Camarero: Juan**
Cliente No.			**Menú**
1 (mujer)	2 (hombre)	3 (niño)	
			Primer Plato
			Sopa de verduras
			Espárragos con mayonesa
			Tomate relleno con pollo
			Segundo Plato
			Ravioles
			Bistec de ternera
			Medio pollo al ajo
			Papas fritas
			Puré de papas
			Ensalada
			Mixta
			Zanahoria y huevo
			Espinacas, queso y tomate

Actividad 7 **Cómo poner la mesa.** You will hear a man on the radio describing how to set a place setting. As you listen to him, draw where each item should go on the place mat.

Actividad 8 **Los preparativos de la fiesta.** Mrs. Uriburu calls home to find out if her husband has already done some things for tonight's dinner. While you listen to Mrs. Uriburu's part of the phone conversation, choose from the list the correct answers her husband gives her.

1. a. Sí, ya la limpié.
   b. Sí, ya lo limpié.
2. a. No, no lo compró.
   b. No, no lo compré.
3. a. No tuviste tiempo.
   b. No tuve tiempo.
4. a. Sí, te la preparé.
   b. Sí, se la preparé.
5. a. Sí, se lo di.
   b. Sí, se los di.
6. a. No, no me llamó.
   b. No, no la llamé.

Actividad 9 **La dieta Kitakilos.**

A. Look at the drawings of María before and after Dr. Popoff's diet. Stop the recording and, under each drawing, write two adjectives that describe her. Also imagine and write two things she does now that she didn't used to do before.

Antes

María era ______________________ y
______________________.

Después

Ahora es ______________________ y
______________________.

Ahora puede ______________________ y
______________________.

Nombre ______________________ Sección ______________ Fecha ____________

B. Now listen to a radio ad on Dr. Popoff's diet and write two things María used to do before the diet and two things she does after the diet. It's not necessary to write all the activities she mentions.

Antes	Después
______________________	______________________
______________________	______________________

Actividad 10 **Los testimonios.** There was a bank robbery yesterday and a detective is questioning three witnesses. Listen to the descriptions the witnesses give and choose the correct drawing of the thief.

❐

❐

❐

Actividad 11 **Un mensaje telefónico.** The bank robber calls his boss at home and leaves her a very important message. Listen and write the message. When you finish, stop the recording and use the letters with numbers underneath them to decipher the secret message that the thief leaves his boss.

Mensaje:

_ _ _ _ _ (8) _ _ _ _ (7, 4, 9). _ _ _ _ _ _ (2, 5, 13)

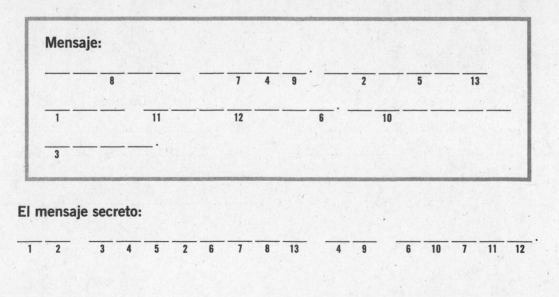

_ _ _ (1) _ _ _ _ _ _ _ (11, 12, 6). _ _ _ _ _ _ (10)

_ _ _ _ (3).

El mensaje secreto:

_ _ (1 2) _ _ _ _ _ _ _ _ (3 4 5 2 6 7 8 13) _ _ (4 9) _ _ _ _ _ (6 10 7 11 12).

Actividad 12 **Los regalos.** María and Pedro are at a sporting goods store that has many items on sale. Listen to their conversation and write what they are going to buy their children.

Le van a comprar a...

1. Miguel ______________________________
2. Felipe ______________________________
3. Ángeles ______________________________
4. Patricia ______________________________

Actividad 13 **Diana en los Estados Unidos.** Diana is talking to Teresa about her life in the U.S. Listen to their conversation and mark whether the following sentences about Diana are true or false.

	Cierto	Falso
1. Vivía en una ciudad pequeña.	❒	❒
2. Enseñaba inglés.	❒	❒
3. Hablaba español casi todo el día.	❒	❒
4. Se levantaba tarde.	❒	❒
5. Ella vivía con sus padres.	❒	❒
6. Estudiaba literatura española.	❒	❒

Conversación: ¡Feliz cumpleaños!
Conversación: Teresa, campeona de tenis

Nombre ______________________ Sección ______________ Fecha ____________

Capítulo 9

Cosas que ocurrieron

Mejora tu pronunciación

The consonants *c*, *s*, and *z*

In Hispanic America, the consonant **c** followed by an *e* or an *i*, and the consonants **s** and **z** are usually pronounced like the *s* in the English word *sin*. In Spain, on the other hand, the consonant **c** followed by an *e* or an *i*, and **z** are usually pronounced like the *th* in the English word *thin*.

Actividad 1 **Escucha y repite.**

A. Listen and repeat the following food-related words. Pay attention to the pronunciation of the consonant **c** followed by an *e* or an *i*, and the consonants **s** and **z**.

1. la taza
2. el vaso
3. el azúcar
4. el tocino
5. la cocina
6. la **cerveza**

B. Now listen to the same words again as they are pronounced by a speaker from Latin America and then by a speaker from Spain. Do not repeat the words.

Actividad 2 **El accidente.** Listen to a Spaniard as he describes an accident he had. Pay attention to the pronunciation of the consonant **c** followed by an *e* or an *i*, and the consonant **z**.

1. Iba a Barcelona, pero tuve un accidente horrible en Zaragoza.
2. Me torcí el tobillo.
3. Luego me corté un dedo y tuve una infección muy grave.
4. Gracias a Dios no me hicieron una operación.
5. Pero ahora tengo un dolor de cabeza muy grande.

Mejora tu comprensión

Actividad 3 No me siento bien.

A. You will hear three conversations about people who have health problems. Listen and write in the chart the problem that each person has.

	Problema
El hombre	
La niña	
Adriana	

B. Now listen to the conversations again and write the solution to each person's problem in the chart below.

	Solución
El hombre	
La niña	
Adriana	

Actividad 4

La conversación telefónica. Clara is talking on the phone with a friend. She has the hiccups and can't finish some phrases. Listen to what Clara says and select a word to complete the idea that she is not able to finish each time her hiccups interrupt her. Number them from 1 to 4.

______ hechos ______ vestidos

______ aburrido ______ preocupada

______ dormidos ______ sentados

Actividad 5

La fiesta inesperada. Esteban decided to have a "come as you are" party yesterday and immediately called his friends to invite them over. Today, Esteban is talking to his mother about the party. Listen to the conversation and mark what the people were doing when Esteban called them.

______ Ricardo a. Estaba mirando televisión.

______ María b. Estaba vistiéndose.

______ Héctor c. Estaba bañándose.

______ Claudia d. Estaba afeitándose.

______ Silvio e. Estaba comiendo.

Nombre ______________ Sección ______________ Fecha ______________

Actividad 6 El accidente automovilístico.

A. You will listen to a radio interview with a doctor who saw an accident between a truck and a school bus. Before listening, stop the recording and use your imagination to write what you think the people from the list were doing when the doctor arrived.

1. los niños ______________
2. los paramédicos ______________
3. la policía ______________
4. los peatones (*pedestrians*) ______________

B. Now listen to the interview and write what the people from the list were doing according to the doctor.

1. los niños ______________
2. los paramédicos ______________
3. la policía ______________
4. los peatones ______________

Actividad 7 Problemas con el carro.

A man had a car accident and is on the phone talking to his car insurance agent about some of the problems his car has. Listen to the conversation and draw an X on the parts of the car that were damaged in the accident.

Actividad 8 Quiero alquilar un carro.

Tomás is in Santiago, Chile, and wants to rent a car for a week to visit the country. Listen to the conversation and complete his notes.

Rent-a-carro: 698–6576

Por semana: $ ______________

Día extra: $ ______________

¿Seguro (*Insurance*) incluido? Sí / No ¿Cuánto? $ ______________

¿Depósito? Sí / No

¿Puedo devolver (*return*) el carro en otra ciudad? Sí / No

¿A qué hora debo devolverlo? ______________

Actividad 9 **La novia de Juan.** Juan is talking to Laura about his girlfriend. Read the questions and then, while you listen to the conversation, answer the questions with complete sentences.

1. ¿Conocía Juan a su novia antes de empezar la universidad? ______________________
2. ¿Cuándo y dónde la conoció? ______________________
3. ¿Qué era algo que no sabía sobre ella cuando empezaron a salir? ______________________
4. ¿Cómo y cuándo lo supo? ______________________
5. ¿Qué piensa hacer Juan? ______________________

Conversación: De vacaciones y enfermo
Conversación: Si manejas, te juegas la vida

Nombre ______________________ Sección ______________ Fecha ____________

Capítulo 10 Mi casa es tu casa

Mejora tu pronunciación

The consonants *g* and *j*

As you saw in Chapter 6, the consonant **g**, when followed by the vowels *a, o,* or *u* or by the vowel combinations *ue* or *ui,* is pronounced a little softer than the *g* in the English word *guy;* for example, **gato, gordo, guerra. G** followed by *e* or *i* and **j** in all positions are both pronounced similarly to the *h* in the English word *hot,* as in the words **general** and **Jamaica.**

Actividad 1 **Escucha y repite.** Escucha y repite las siguientes palabras. Presta atención a la pronunciación de las consonantes **g** y **j.**

1. ojo
2. Juan Carlos
3. trabajar
4. escoger
5. congelador
6. gigante

Actividad 2 **Las asignaturas.** Escucha y repite la siguiente conversación del libro entre dos estudiantes. Presta atención a la pronunciación de las consonantes **g** y **j.**

ESTUDIANTE 1 ¿Qué asignatura vas a escoger?

ESTUDIANTE 2 Creo que psicología.

ESTUDIANTE 1 Pero es mejor geografía.

ESTUDIANTE 2 ¡Ay! Pero no traje el papel para inscribirme.

ESTUDIANTE 1 ¿El papel rojo?

ESTUDIANTE 2 No. El papel anaranjado.

Mejora tu comprensión

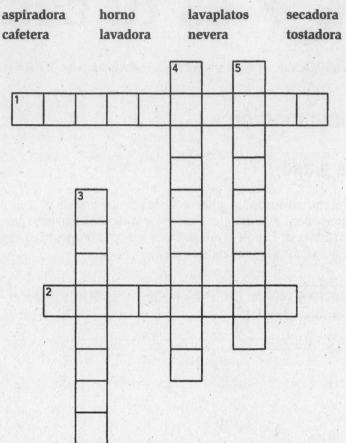

Actividad 3 **El crucigrama.** Usa las pistas (*clues*) que escuchas para completar el crucigrama sobre aparatos electrodomésticos *(electrical appliances)*. Mira la lista de palabras y el crucigrama antes de empezar.

aspiradora	**horno**	**lavaplatos**	**secadora**
cafetera	**lavadora**	**nevera**	**tostadora**

1
2
3
4
5

Actividad 4 **En busca de apartamento.** Paulina ve el anuncio de un apartamento para alquilar y llama para averiguar más información. Escucha la conversación entre Paulina y el dueño del apartamento y completa sus apuntes.

Teléfono 986-4132
Apartamento: 1 dormitorio
¿Alquiler? $ ________ ¿Depósito? $ ________
¿Amueblado? ________ ¿Luz natural? ________
Baño: ¿bañera? ________ ¿bidé? ________
¿Dirección? San Martín ________ ¿Piso? ________

Nombre ______________________ Sección ______________ Fecha ____________

Actividad 5 **¿Dónde ponemos los muebles?** Paulina y su esposo van a vivir en un nuevo apartamento y ahora planean en qué parte de la habitación van a poner cada mueble. Mientras escuchas la conversación, indica dónde van a poner cada mueble. Pon el número de cada cosa en uno de los cuadrados (*squares*) del plano de la habitación.

1 alfombra	**3 cómoda**	**5 sillón**
2 cama	**4 mesa**	**6 televisor**

6

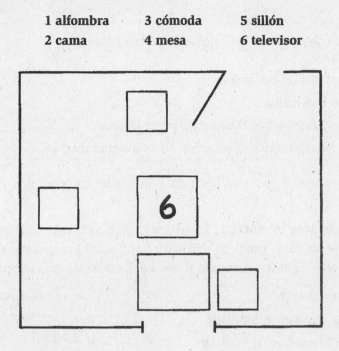

Actividad 6 **En el Rastro.** Vicente y Teresa van al Rastro (un mercado al aire libre en Madrid) para buscar unos estantes baratos. Escucha la conversación con el vendedor y, basándote en lo que escuchas, marca si las oraciones son ciertas o falsas.

	Cierto	Falso
1. Hay poca gente en este mercado.	❐	❐
2. Vicente ve unos estantes.	❐	❐
3. Los estantes son baratos.	❐	❐
4. Teresa regatea (*bargains*).	❐	❐
5. El comerciante no baja el precio.	❐	❐
6. Teresa compra dos estantes.	❐	❐

Actividad 7 **Radio consulta.**

A. Esperanza es la conductora del programa de radio "Problemas". Escucha la conversación entre Esperanza y una persona que la llama para contarle un problema y marca cuál es su problema.

1. ❐ La señora está deprimida (*depressed*).
2. ❐ La señora no sabe dónde está su animal.
3. ❐ La señora tiene un esposo que no se baña.
4. ❐ La señora tiene un hijo sucio (*dirty*).

Continúa en la página siguiente →

B. Antes de escuchar la respuesta de Esperanza, escoge y marca bajo "Tus consejos" qué consejos de la lista te gustaría darle a la persona.

	Tus consejos	Los consejos de Esperanza
1. Debe poner a su esposo en la bañera.	❐	❐
2. Debe hablar con un compañero de trabajo de su esposo para que él le hable a su esposo.	❐	❐
3. Debe llevar a su esposo a un psicólogo.	❐	❐
4. Ella debe hablar con una amiga.	❐	❐
5. Tiene que decirle a su esposo que él es muy desconsiderado.	❐	❐
6. Tiene que decirle a su esposo que la situación no puede continuar así.	❐	❐

C. Ahora escucha a Esperanza y marca en la última columna los tres consejos que ella le da.

Actividad 8 **El mensaje telefónico.** La jefa de Patricio salió de la oficina y le dejó un mensaje telefónico para recordarle las cosas que tiene que hacer hoy. Escucha el mensaje y escribe una **P** delante de las cosas que ella le pide a Patricio que haga y una **J** delante de las cosas que va a hacer la jefa.

1. ______ comprar una cafetera
2. ______ escribirle un email al Sr. Montero
3. ______ llamar al Sr. Montero para verificar su dirección de email
4. ______ llamar a la agencia de viajes
5. ______ ir a la agencia de viajes
6. ______ ir al banco
7. ______ pagar el pasaje

Actividad 9 **Busco un hombre/una mujer...**

A. Vas a escuchar un anuncio en la radio de una mujer que busca su compañero ideal. Antes de escuchar el anuncio, para la grabación (*recording*) y marca las características que buscas en un compañero o una compañera.

Busco/Busca un hombre/una mujer...	**tú**	**ella**
que sea inteligente	_____	_____
que tenga dinero	_____	_____
que tenga un trabajo estable (*stable*)	_____	_____
que salga por la noche	_____	_____
que sepa bailar	_____	_____
que sea guapo/a	_____	_____
que sea simpático/a	_____	_____

B. Ahora escucha el anuncio en la radio y marca en la lista de arriba las características que busca esta mujer en un hombre.

Conversación: En busca de apartamento
Conversación: Todos son expertos

Capítulo 11 El tiempo libre

Mejora tu pronunciación

The consonant *h*

The consonant **h** is always silent in Spanish. For example, the word *hotel* in English is **hotel** in Spanish.

Actividad 1 **Escucha y repite.** Escucha y repite las siguientes palabras relacionadas con la salud.

1. **h**emorragia
2. **h**ospital
3. **h**acer un análisis
4. **h**erida
5. alco**h**ol
6. **h**epatitis

Actividad 2 **La conversación.** Escucha y repite las siguientes oraciones de la conversación en el libro de texto entre Rosa y Raúl.

1. Es que los **h**ombres son más fuertes.
2. Hay algunas diferencias entre la Ka**h**lo y yo, empezando con mi **h**abilidad artística.
3. Hacen falta las manos y no los músculos.
4. Tenían **h**ijos de menos de cinco años.

Mejora tu comprensión

Actividad 3 **¿Certeza o duda?** Vas a escuchar cuatro oraciones. Para cada una, indica si la persona expresa certeza o duda.

	Certeza	Duda
1.	❒	❒
2.	❒	❒
3.	❒	❒
4.	❒	❒

Actividad 4 **¿Quién las hace?** Escucha a cuatro personas e indica, en cada caso, si la persona expresa emoción por sus acciones o las acciones que hacen otras personas.

	Acciones de la persona que habla	Acciones de otra persona
1.	❐	❐
2.	❐	❐
3.	❐	❐
4.	❐	❐

Actividad 5 **Mañana es día de fiesta.** Silvia habla por teléfono con una amiga sobre sus planes para mañana. Mientras escuchas lo que dice, escribe cuatro oraciones sobre lo que quizás ocurra.

Mañana quizá / tal vez...

1. ______________________________
2. ______________________________
3. ______________________________
4. ______________________________

Actividad 6 **La receta de doña Petrona.** Vas a escuchar a doña Petrona mientras demuestra en su programa de televisión, **"Recetas exitosas"**, cómo preparar una ensalada de papas. Mientras escuchas la descripción de cada paso, numera los dibujos en el orden apropiado. ¡Ojo! Hay algunos dibujos extras.

______ ______ ______ ______

______ ______ ______ ______

Nombre ______________________ Sección ______________ Fecha ____________

Actividad 7 **Un regalo poco común.** Antes de escuchar el siguiente anuncio de la radio, escribe un regalo poco común *(unusual)* que alguna vez le diste a un amigo o amiga. Luego lee la información que se presenta y escucha el anuncio para completarla.

regalo que diste: ______________________

1. tipo de regalo: ______________________
2. precio: ______________________
3. algo para beber: ______________________
4. dos cosas para comer: ______________________
5. otra cosa (no bebida o comida): ______________________
6. dónde comprar el regalo: ______________________

Actividad 8 **Un anuncio informativo.**

A. Antes de escuchar un anuncio informativo para padres, lee la siguiente lista de pasatiempos. Marca, en la columna que dice **tú**, qué actividades hacías tú cuando eras niño o niña.

	tú	**el anuncio**
1. coleccionar algo	____	____
2. hacer artesanías	____	____
3. hacer crucigramas	____	____
4. hacer rompecabezas	____	____
5. jugar al ajedrez	____	____
6. jugar con juegos electrónicos	____	____
7. jugar juegos de mesa	____	____
8. navegar por Internet	____	____
9. pescar	____	____
10. tejer	____	____

B. Ahora escucha el anuncio y marca en la lista de arriba las actividades que los padres les pueden enseñar a sus hijos según lo que dice el anuncio.

Actividad 9 **Cuando estudio mucho.**

A. Antes de escuchar una conversación entre tres amigos, escribe en español tres cosas que te gusta hacer cuando tienes tiempo libre.

1. ____
2. ____
3. ____

Continúa en la página siguiente →

B. Federico, Gustavo y Marisa están hablando de las cosas que les gusta hacer cuando tienen tiempo libre. Escucha la conversación y escribe oraciones para indicar qué actividad o actividades le gusta hacer a cada uno.

1. Federico: ______________________________
____
2. Gustavo: ______________________________
____
3. Marisa: ______________________________
____

Actividad 10 **El viaje a Machu Picchu.** El Sr. López recibe una llamada. Antes de escuchar, lee las oraciones. Luego, escucha la conversación y marca si las siguientes oraciones son ciertas o falsas.

	Cierto	Falso
1. El señor López ganó un viaje a Ecuador.	❐	❐
2. La señora dice que una computadora escogió su número de teléfono.	❐	❐
3. La señora dice que él ganó pasajes para dos personas.	❐	❐
4. El señor López le da su número de tarjeta de crédito a la mujer.	❐	❐
5. El señor López cree que la mujer le dice la verdad.	❐	❐

Conversación: El trabajo y el tiempo libre
Conversación: Después de comer, nada mejor que la sobremesa

Nombre ______________________ Sección ______________ Fecha __________

Capítulo 12 ¡Viva la música!

Mejora tu pronunciación

Linking

In normal conversation, you link words as you speak to provide a smooth transition from one word to the next. In Spanish, the last letter of a word can usually be linked to the first letter of the following word, for example, **mis‿amigas, tú‿y‿yo.** When the last letter of a word is the same as the first letter of the following word, they are pronounced as one letter, for example, **las‿sillas, te‿encargo.** Remember that the *h* is silent in Spanish, so the link occurs as follows: **la‿habilidad.**

Actividad 1 **Escucha y repite.** Escucha y repite las siguientes frases prestando atención al unir las palabras.

1. la‿cartera
2. mandar‿un‿email
3. la‿estampilla
4. caerse‿el‿servidor
5. el‿enlace
6. no quiero‿hacer‿esa‿cola

Actividad 2 **En el restaurante argentino.** Escucha y repite parte de la conversación entre Teresa y Vicente en el restaurante argentino.

VICENTE Espero que‿a la‿experta de tenis le gusten la comida‿y los tangos‿argentinos con bandoneón‿y todo.

TERESA Los tangos que cantaba Carlos Gardel me fascinan. El‿otro día, bajé de‿Internet "Mi Buenos‿Aires Querido" cuando yo te vuelva‿a ver... Pero, dime Vicente, ¿cómo‿encontraste‿este restaurante?

VICENTE Navegando por‿Internet. Bajé‿una lista de restaurantes‿argentinos y‿este tenía muy buenos comentarios.

Mejora tu comprensión

Actividad 3 **Los instrumentos musicales.** Vas a escuchar cuatro instrumentos musicales. Numera cada instrumento que escuches.

______ batería

______ violín

______ violonchelo

______ trompeta

______ flauta

Actividad 4 **Tengo correo electrónico.** Escucha la conversación telefónica entre Fernando y Betina y completa la tabla del manual.

Dirección de correo electrónico de Betina: ____________________
Sitio que recomienda Fernando: ____________________

Actividad 5 **¿De qué hablan?** Antes de escuchar, para la grabación y mira la siguiente lista. Luego, escucha cinco miniconversaciones e indica de qué o de quién se habla en cada caso.

______ el buzón

______ el/la cartero/a

______ la estampilla

______ hacer la cola

______ mandar un fax

______ el paquete

______ el remite

______ las tarjetas postales

Actividad 6 **La isla Pita Pita.** Escucha la descripción de la isla Pita Pita y usa los símbolos que se presentan y los nombres de los lugares para completar el mapa incompleto. Los nombres de los lugares que se mencionan son **Blanca Nieves, Hércules, Mala-Mala, Panamericana** y **Pata.**

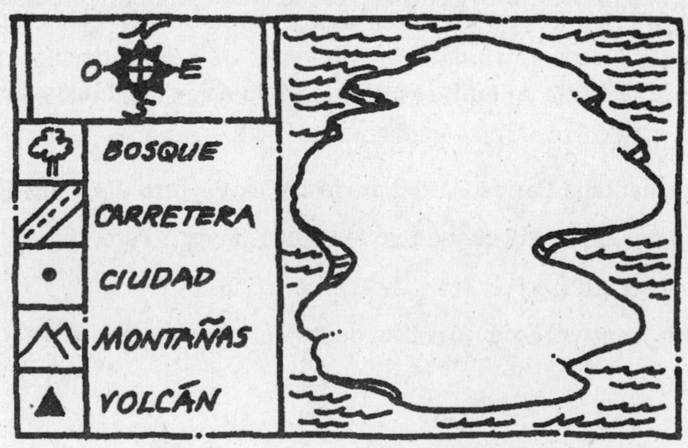

Nombre ______________________ Sección ______________ Fecha __________

Actividad 7 **Visite Venezuela.** ¿Sabes cuáles de los lugares de la lista forman parte de Venezuela y cuáles no? Escucha el anuncio comercial sobre Venezuela y marca solo los lugares que pertenecen a ese país.

______ el salto Ángel

______ las cataratas del Iguazú

______ la Ciudad Bolívar

______ Mérida

______ las islas Galápagos

______ las islas Los Roques

______ las playas de Punta del Este

______ la playa de La Guaira

______ el volcán de Fuego

Actividad 8 **La dieta.**

A. La Sra. Kilomás necesita bajar de peso (*to lose weight*) y está en el consultorio hablando con el médico. Antes de escuchar, escribe tres cosas que crees que el médico le va a decir que no coma.

1. ______________ 2. ______________ 3. ______________

B. Ahora escucha la conversación y escribe en la columna correcta las cosas que la Sra. Kilomás puede y no puede comer o beber.

Coma:	**No coma:**
______________	______________
______________	______________
	______________
	______________
	______________

Beba:	**No beba:**
______________	______________
______________	
______________	

Actividad 9 **La llamada anónima.** Unos hombres secuestraron (*kidnapped*) al Sr. Tomono, un diplomático, en Guayaquil, Ecuador, y quieren un millón de dólares. Llaman a la Sra. Tomono para decirle qué debe hacer con el dinero. Antes de escuchar, lee las oraciones que aparecen en el manual. Luego, escucha la conversación telefónica y marca si las siguientes oraciones son ciertas o falsas.

	Cierto	**Falso**
1. La Sra. Tomono debe poner el dinero en una mochila marrón.	☐	☐
2. Ella debe ir a la esquina (*corner*) de las calles Quito y Colón.	☐	☐
3. Tiene que hablar por un teléfono público.	☐	☐
4. Tiene que ir en taxi.	☐	☐

Actividad 10 **Pichicho.** Sebastián le está mostrando a su amigo Ramón las cosas que su perro Pichicho puede hacer. Escucha a Sebastián y numera los dibujos según las órdenes. ¡Ojo! Hay dibujos de ocho órdenes pero Sebastián solo da seis.

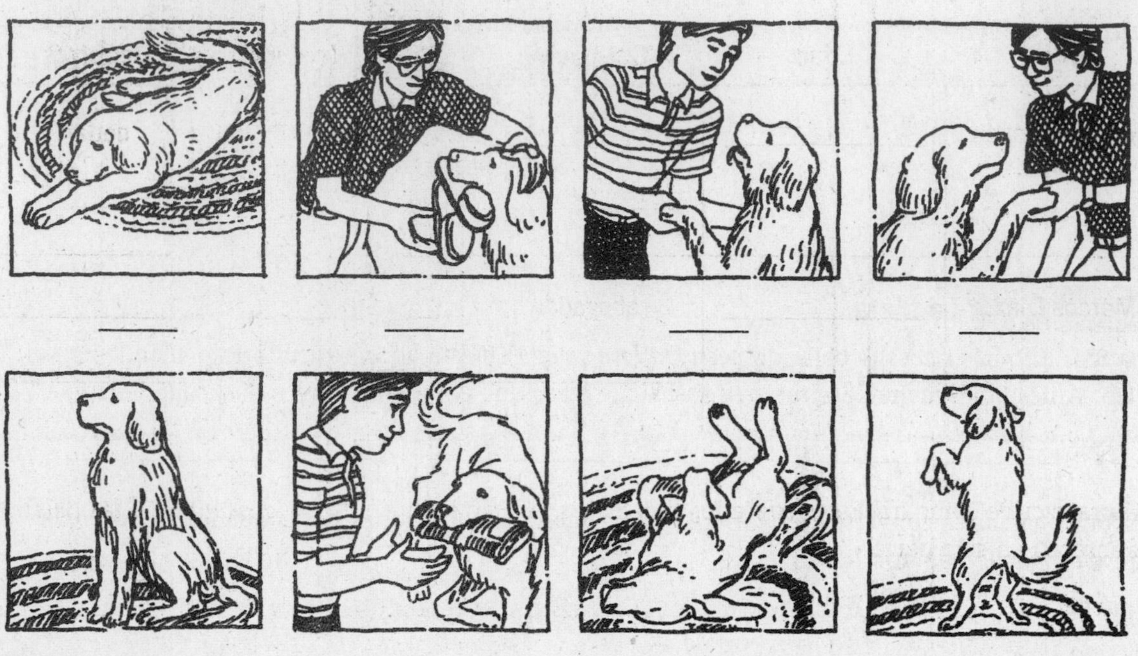

Actividad 11 **Las tres casas.**

A. Llamas a una inmobiliaria (*real-estate agency*) para obtener información sobre tres casas y te contesta el contestador automático. Escucha la descripción de las casas y completa la tabla.

	Tamaño (m2)	Dormitorios	Año	Precio (dólares)
Casa 1	250			350.000
Casa 2		2		
Casa 3			2005	

B. Ahora mira la tabla y escucha las siguientes oraciones. Marca **C** si son ciertas o **F** si son falsas.

1. ______
2. ______
3. ______
4. ______
5. ______

Nombre ______________________ Sección ______________ Fecha ___________

Actividad 12 La peluquería.

A. La Sra. López y la Sra. Díaz están en la peluquería hablando de sus hijos. Escucha la conversación y completa la información sobre sus hijos.

Hijo	Edad	Ocupación	Sueldo (*salary*)	Deportes
Alejandro López	________	________ ________	________	nadar ________
Marcos Díaz	________	abogado y ________	________	________ ________

B. Ahora escribe comparaciones sobre los dos chicos usando la información de la tabla y las palabras que aparecen en esta parte.

1. joven: ______________________________
2. activo: ______________________________
3. ganar dinero: ______________________________

Conversación: ¡Qué música!
Conversación: La propuesta